Collection of **The National Quilt Museum**

COVER IMAGE: Detail, ESCAPADE by Libby Lehman, Houston, TX. For the full quilt image, go to page 139.

ACKNOWLEDGMENTS

Great appreciation is due to
Charles R. Lynch for his excellent photography throughout the book,
to Judy Schwender, the Museum's Curator of Collections,
for the work of maintaining collection records,
and to Angela Schade for graphic design.

DEDICATION

This book is dedicated to our founders Bill and Meredith Schroeder. In 1991 the museum was opened to Honor Today's Quilter, exhibiting contemporary quilts year round. We can not thank them enough for their passion and tireless effort on behalf of today's quilting community. We are honored to continue their vision.

We would also like to dedicate this book to all of the wonderful quilters whose work is exhibited in the Museum. We are honored to share their work with the world.

Contents

ABOUT US

Advancing the Art...

Founded in 1991, The National Quilt Museum works to advance the art of today's quilters by bringing it to new and expanding audiences worldwide. We serve the quilting community by providing in-facility and travelling exhibits, youth and adult educational programs, and advocacy efforts.

The National Quilt Museum is the world's largest museum devoted to quilt and fiber art. A destination for quilters and art enthusiasts worldwide, annually the Museum receives visitors from all 50 US states and over 45 foreign countries from every continent. The Museum's in-facility and travelling exhibits are viewed by over 110,000 people per year. In addition, over 4,000 youth and adults participate in Museum youth and adult educational opportunities on an annual basis.

Located in a 27,000 square foot facility in historic downtown Paducah, Kentucky, the Museum's three galleries feature exhibits of the finest quilt and fiber art in the world. The Museum's vibrant and breathtaking exhibits are rotated 8-10 times per year. The primary gallery, with over 7,000 square feet of exhibit space, features quilts from the Museum's collections which includes over 400 works of art. The two other galleries feature unique and diverse travelling exhibits.

The Museum has also gained a reputation for its educational programs. Throughout the year, the Museum hosts educational programs on a diverse number of topics for quilters of all skill sets. Quilters come from all over the world to attend the Museum's educational programs taught by master quilters.

The Museum's youth education programs are attended by over 4,000 young people of all ages. Several of these programs have received national media attention. The School Block Challenge, sponsored by Moda Fabrics, is an annual contest in which participants are challenged to make a quilt block out of a packet of three fabrics. This program continues to be utilized by schools and community organizations as part of their art curricula in over 20 states. Other popular youth programs include the annual Quilt Camp for Kids, Kidz Day in the Arts, and the Junior Quilters and Textile Artists Club.

NOTE FROM THE CEO

Frank Bennett

I was first introduced to quilting about six years ago. I was a writer and consultant living in Dallas, Texas and I had been hired to do a project for the Museum. I must admit that I had some of the same perceptions that many people unfamiliar with the artform hold. I remember having a few quilts in my house as a kid, but that was really my only experience. I still remember the first time I stepped into the galleries. To say that I was completely amazed by the beauty of the artwork around me would be an understatement. It was really much more a spiritual experience. I completely got lost in the experience. At the time, I had no idea that the experience would change the path of my life.

A few years later when the Museum's previous director retired I decided to make a career change. I'll occasionally have people ask me how I could walk away from a lucrative consulting business that I had spent years developing, but from my perception, I don't see how anyone would not have if they had the same choice. I start every day by taking a few minutes before the Museum opens and walk through some of the most extraordinary art in the world. I meet visitors literally from every state in the US and countries on every continent. Every day I get to interact with other people experiencing quilting for the first time. Not to mention that the quilters the Museum represents are some of the kindest and most talented people I have ever met.

The National Quilt Museum works to advance the art of today's quilters by bringing it to new and expanding audiences worldwide. As CEO, while I wear a lot of hats, my purpose is quite simple: I work to make it possible for every single person on earth to experience the work of today's quilters for themselves just like I did the first time I came through the Museum doors.

I'm honored to serve the wonderfully talented quilting community.

Verla Hale ADAMS & Mary Carol GOBLE

Trip Around the World
105" x 108", Mary Carol Goble, Nephi, UT, and Verla Hale Adams, Oakley, ID, 1985.
Cottons and cotton blends; machine pieced and hand quilted.
1997.06.86

Quilting was a matter of providing warmth and love for her family for Verla. It was also a family effort; for many years, she quilted "beautiful pieced tops" made by her daughter, Mary Carol Goble.

Verla Hale Adams

I hope to inspire people to try anything creative that will make them feel good about themselves. Quiltmaking has been a great comfort to me.

Mary Carol Goble

DAWN AMOS

Having learned how to make quilts from her Sioux in-laws, especially in the Broken Star pattern, Dawn found artistry and achievement later when she began dyeing her own fabrics.

THE BEGINNINGS
64" x 84", Dawn Amos, Rapid City, SD, 1990. Cottons, hand dyed; hand appliquéd and hand quilted.
1996.01.05

AWARDS:
AQS
Best of Show
1990

DAWN AMOS

DESCENDING VISIONS
46" x 62", Dawn Amos, Rapid City, SD, 1992. Hand-dyed cottons; hand appliquéd and hand quilted.
1996.01.09

AWARDS:
RJR
Best Wall Quilt
1992

DAWN AMOS

AWARDS:
RJR
Best Wall Quilt
1989

LOOKING BACK ON BROKEN PROMISES
53" x 38", Dawn Amos, Rapid City, SD, 1989. Cottons, hand dyed; hand appliquéd and hand quilted.
1996.01.16

Charlotte WARR ANDERSEN

THREE FOR THE CROWN
54" x 54", Charlotte Warr Andersen, Salt Lake City, UT, 1987. Silks; hand pieced and hand quilted.
1997.06.83

Charlotte is best known for her highly realistic, original, unique pictorial quilts. A popular and effective teacher, she enjoys making quilts that connect with American history.

AWARDS:
First Place
Wall Quilt, Professional
1987

Faye Anderson

The only reason I have ever made a quilt or other art work was to see how it would come out, to see if I had the skills to create what was in my mind's eye.

Each project would have to be challenging because if I were already certain of the outcome, it wouldn't be fun to make.

The surprises and discoveries of the creative process are the payoff, more so than the finished piece.

Garden Party
83" x 98½", Faye Anderson, Boulder, CO, 1987. Cottons; machine pieced, hand appliquéd, hand embroidered, and hand quilted.
1992.05.01

FAYE ANDERSON

SPRING WINDS
76" x 87", Faye Anderson, Boulder, CO, 1986. Cottons; hand appliquéd and hand quilted.
1996.01.24

AWARDS:
AQS Best of Show
1986

JANICE ANTHONY

Janice brings her painter's eye for color to her fabric choices. She finds artistry in the interplay of light and color and achievement in the technical challenges of good workmanship.

INCANTATION,
29" x 44", Janice Anthony, Jackson, ME, 1984. Cottons, painted silk; hand and machine pieced, and hand quilted. 1997.06.29

Virginia Avery

When I started my career I simply wanted to make quilts and one-of-a-kind clothing well enough that I would be asked to teach.

I wanted my personal stamp on everything I made, and I wanted to help my students draw on their own resources—develop an idea or inspiration, choose the colors and techniques, and follow their own creativity in producing the very best work they could. When this has been accomplished, affirmation and satisfaction naturally follow.

Quiltmaking taxes creativity. We are somehow compelled to go through the "what if?" process to see what happens. Eventually, we leave our mark on line, function, form, color, and texture. There is endless excitement to this process and endless satisfaction in its completion.

Move Over Matisse I
36" x 70", Virginia Avery, Port Chester, NY, 1980. Cottons; hand appliquéd and hand quilted.
2001.01.01

IRIS AYCOCK

Iris is well-known for her leaf print quilts, wallhangings, and framed pieces. A member of the Southern Highland Craft Guild, she spends her time concentrating on creating her pieces. Hammering, dyeing, and weaving techniques inform the organic look of her work.

AWARDS:
RJR
Best Wall Quilt
1994

HAMMERED AT HOME
77" x 78", Iris Aycock, Woodville, AL, 1994. Cottons; machine pieced and machine quilted.
1996.01.13

Marilyn BADGER & Claudia Clark MYERS

Greensleeves
74" x 80", Marilyn Badger and Claudia Clark Myers, Duluth, MN, 2008. Cottons, silk, linen, cotton batting; machine pieced, long-arm machine quilted.
2009.01.04

"Marilyn Badger and I love working in silk," writes Claudia Clark Myers, "so when I found the green and earth tone Dupioni silks that went so well with an antique silk brocade I'd been saving for something special, I knew this was 'it'. As the design came together, it began to take on a medieval look---Sherwood Forest comes to mind---but I added the appliqué flowers and leaves to soften the angularity. Marilyn designed unique quilting patterns that could be overlaid on the Compass piecing, to create a three-dimensional layered and gold lace look."

AWARDS:
Gammill Longarm Machine Quilting
2009

BARBARA BARBER

The numerous challenges inherent in making quilts appeal to Barbara, whether working in a color unusual for her, entering a competition, or making a quilt within a certain time frame. Teaching others is a vital part of passing along her self-taught machine-quilting skills.

AWARDS:

Bernina

Machine Workmanship

1996

GOATO AND FRIENDS

83" x 83", Barbara Barber, Andover, Hants, England, 1995. Cottons; machine appliquéd, machine quilted, and machine embroidered.

1996.02.01

Sonya Lee Barrington

Bed Quilt #1
87" x 92½", Sonya Lee Barrington, San Francisco, CA, c. 1992. Cottons; machine pieced. Machine quilted by Dorrie Whipple, Cotati, CA.
2007.13.01

When talking about my work, I usually call myself a craftsperson using the medium of the quilt to create high-end, functional and/or decorative items.

It is imperative to please myself by making the very best technical and artistic statement possible no matter the material, be it hand-dyed cotton, recycled wool, or silk. The techniques that I use must allow me to achieve this goal.

I hope to seriously engage each viewer so that she or he experiences my work to the fullest. I also hope to inspire my viewers to create work that is gratifying to them.

SUE BENNER

"A cell can be described as the functional unit of a larger whole," writes Sue Benner. "I think about cells as an organizing device in many contexts, but the biological cell is a particular source of fascination for me. These shapes live in my mind and are the building blocks of my world and my art."

While pursuing a degree in molecular biology and masters in biomedical illustration, Sue Benner created her vision of the microscopic universe in painted and quilted textile constructions. Her early work propelled her to become a studio artist in 1980, working primarily in the medium which later became known as the Art Quilt.

Sue is an innovator in her field, creating original dyed and painted fabrics which she combines with recycled textiles to form fields of structured pattern, vivid beauty, and riotous variation.

CELLULAR STRUCTURE VI (STACK OF SIX)
40" x 81¼", Sue Benner, Dallas, TX, 2007. Silk, cotton, polyester, commercial and found fabrics, recycled clothing, dye, paint; machine pieced, machine quilted.
2011.02.01

Cletha Bird

Inspired by Grace McCance Snyder's needlepoint-like Flower Basket quilt, Cletha set out to make a one-of-a-kind quilt of her own.

"Had I known more about the challenges of quiltmaking, I am sure that I would not have tried that design!"—especially for a first quilt, which is what this work was.

Flower Basket
96" x 104", Cletha Bird, Columbus, IN, 1987. Cottons and cotton blends; machine pieced and hand quilted.
1997.06.22

JANE BLAIR

Except to aim for good design and color, there are no goals to my quiltmaking other than to satisfy my need for a creative outlet.

I've done the teaching, lectures, and shows. I've won many awards, but nothing achieves satisfaction like the joy of actually creating something tangible from that idea in your head.

GYPSY IN MY SOUL
66" x 84", Jane Blair, Wyomissing, PA, 1987. Cottons and cotton/polyesters; hand pieced, hand appliquéd, and hand quilted. Named one of the 100 Best American Quilts of the 20th Century.
1996.01.12

AWARDS:
AQS Best of Show
1988

Jane Blair

Morisco
80" x 90", Jane Blair, Wyomissing, PA, 1984. Cottons and cotton/polyester blends; hand pieced and hand quilted.
1997.06.40

JANE BLAIR

NIGHT BLOOM
56" x 72", Jane Blair, Wyomissing, PA, 1985. Cottons and cotton/polyesters; hand pieced and hand quilted.
1997.06.46

AWARDS:
First Place
Wall Quilt, Professional
1986

Jane Blair

Raggedy Sun Worshippers
48" x 64", Jane Blair, Wyomissing, PA, 1996. Cottons, cotton/polyesters; hand appliquéd, hand and machine pieced, and hand quilted.
1996.04.01

Awards:
RJR
Best Wall Quilt
1996

Judi Warren Blaydon

My quilts are visual diaries that reflect what I love and record what I remember. They are personal recollections in quilt form, expressed abstractly rather than pictorially.

So while my work contains allusions to content that may, at first, be meaningful only to me, I always hope that color and composition will somehow convey that content, in a way that will intrigue—or at least attract—the viewer's interest and appreciation.

What I hope to achieve is the empathy and involvement of viewers by evoking a response that allows them to discover their own meaning, that evokes a memory of their own, that inspires a kind of "conversation without words,"—a collaboration between the quiltmaker and the observer.

The Mountain and the Magic: Night Lights
65" x 65", Judi Warren Blaydon, Milford, MI, 1995. Lamé, rayon, American and Japanese cottons, antique kimono silk; machine pieced, hand quilted, hand appliquéd, and hand beaded.
2001.02.01

Arleen Boyd

Roses by Starlight
89" x 100½", Arleen Boyd, Rochester, NY, 1985. Cottons; machine pieced and hand quilted.
1997.06.66

Quiltmaking offers the opportunity to combine comfort with artistry.

My first introduction to it was in visiting my prospective in-laws in Pennsylvania. They were prime examples of thrift and made quilts for use, but as lovely as possible with what they had on hand, usually scraps from home sewing.

Now that we are grandparents there are added opportunities to supply quilts for cuddling, which provides pleasure in the making and in seeing them used.

Because of the friendships formed in quilt clubs and at shows, my life is enriched by sharing ideas and working with others who enjoy the same activity.

Francis Abell Brand

Frances Abell Brand developed a love of sewing at an early age. This, coupled with her mastery of a variety of early American decorative art techniques, has inspired her to create more than 85 quilts.

The central image and four smaller images in the inner border are theorem paintings, created with layers of stencils on velvet. The technique became popular in the 1800s as it was taught in girl's academies. Frances learned the technique while a member of The Historical Society of Early American Decoration.

"I love to look at and examine antique quilts," writes Frances. "They create warmth and a sense of comfort. I appreciate the artistry, creativity, and workmanship demonstrated by the early quilt makers. They created beautiful quilts by doing much with little."

Fruitorama
79" x 79", Francis Abell Brand, West Dennis, MA, 1998. Cottons, velvet; machine pieced, hand stencil painted, hand appliquéd, hand quilted.
2011.10.01

Elizabeth Brimelow

I have to ask myself, why if I can draw and paint, do I work with cloth? I think the answer has to be that the cloth itself adds another dimension to the work – it is not just the medium on which the image is placed. I use cloth for its tactile qualities. I love the intimacy of hand stitching and I also like the substance of large pieces of fabric. Traditional techniques are part of the 'tools of the trade' for any quiltmaker. I use several traditional techniques in my work, but have never made a traditional quilt. All my work starts with observational drawing.

Peach, Pear, Plum
55" x 60", Elizabeth Brimelow, Macclesfield, UK, 2006. Silk, Cotton, silk metallic organza, Bondaweb; reverse appliqué, hand stitching, machine stitching, hand seed stitching. RIGHT: Reverse side of Peach, Pear, Plum
2010.12.01

BECKY BROWN

I was born to sew and quilt. Quiltmaking is the creative outlet to explore the endless design and color ideas I have, to experiment with and learn from as my ideas grow.

It's more than just the design and the color; the hand quilting soothes my soul and frees my mind.

Over the decades I have achieved recognition and numerous awards, which validate my quilts; however my greatest achievements in quiltmaking are the many friends that I have made along the way and knowing that my children and grandchildren sleep under quilts stitched with love, just the way I did when I was a child.

AWARDS:

First Place,
Innovative Pieced, Professional
1995

DREAMCATCHER
66" x 82", Becky Brown, Richmond, VA, 1994. Cottons; hand pieced, hand appliquéd, hand quilted.
1997.07.08

Nancy S. Brown

Mount Pleasant Miners
48" x 55", Nancy S. Brown, Oakland, CA, 1993. Cottons, hand dyed and painted; hand appliquéd, machine pieced, and hand quilted.
1996.01.20

Ultimately, I hope that my quilts will be around for a long time and will become a part of how I leave my mark on this earth.

As for right now, I hope that both my family and animal quilts bring some enjoyment to their viewers.

I also hope that my animal quilts help their viewers become more aware of the beauty and importance of animals in this world.

Awards:
RJR
Best Wall Quilt
1993

Bonnie K. Browning

I have been quilting for thirty years, but my love of needlework and sewing began as a small child using my mother's treadle sewing machine. From making Christmas ornaments to my first formal sewing instruction to completing my first quilt in the 1970s, I have enjoyed every part of the process—designing, choosing fabrics, stitching, and completing the projects.

As a visual person, I see quilt patterns and quilting designs everywhere that I travel. My inspiration comes from a field of wild flowers, clouds in the sky, or the birds in our backyard. With photography as my hobby, I am known to record hundreds of photographs during my trips to use as design sources in my work.

AWARDS:

Third Place Award

Other Techniques, Amateur

1986

A Little Bit of Candlewicking

64" x 97", Bonnie K. Browning, Paducah, KY, 1983. Unbleached muslin, Cluny lace and satin ribbon; candlewicked, machine pieced, and hand quilted. 1997.06.33

Barbara Brunner

Barbara creates virtual flower gardens by making roses and tulips come alive in her quilt art.

Quilting is how she expresses her feelings and ideas, and she tries to quilt every day.

Roses for a June Bride
84" x 109", Barbara Brunner, Schofield, WI, 1986. Cottons; hand appliquéd and hand quilted.
1997.06.67

CYNTHIA BUETTNER

CROSSINGS
64" x 52", Cynthia Buettner, Hilliard, OH, 1986.
Hand-dyed cottons; machine pieced and hand quilted.
1997.06.15

With a great-grandmother described as a master quilter, Cynthia grew up fascinated by quilts. She has taught, designed her own fabrics, and sold hand-dyed fabrics around the world.

Melinda Bula

When Melinda Bula's son (and only child) decided to join the Marines after college, she made this quilt to deal with her emotions. The image depicts our flag, tattered but still flying, above a battlefield, and Melinda lovingly dedicates it to all military families.

"It's a painting without any paint," she says, "where every color change is another piece of fabric."

"I started to take the quilt with me on the road when I did trunk shows around the country," writes Melinda. "I had no idea the emotion it would cause in others as I showed it. It was overwhelming and very special, so this quilt is for all the mothers and fathers and brothers and sisters of soldiers through all the wars who, like me, have given their loved ones for our country to be free. This quilt is not mine, it's ours!"

...and Our Flag Was Still There

55½" x 33¾", Melinda Bula, El Dorado Hills, CA, 2011. Rayon 30 weight thread, cottons, cottons hand-dyed by the artist, Quilters Dream 100% cotton batting, raw-edge machine appliqué, machine quilted.
2013.02.01

Moneca Calvert

Moneca's designs and workmanship are recognized worldwide, and she has traveled the globe teaching contemporary quiltmaking for almost three decades.

Neon Nights
53" x 53", Moneca Calvert, Reno, NV, 1986. Cottons, cotton blends; machine pieced and hand quilted.
1997.06.43

ELSIE M. CAMPBELL

STAR FLOWER

83" x 83", Elsie M. Campbell, Dodge City, KS, 2002. Cottons; machine pieced, machine appliquéd, and hand quilted. National Quilting Association Masterpiece Quilt. 2003.03.01

I love to make traditional quilts with contemporary twists. The twist may come from using new color combinations, or from adding a little appliqué or paint to traditional pieced blocks.

Most recently, I've discovered that simple blocks are more versatile than complicated ones. By utilizing highly contrasting fabrics or more subtle color and value changes, it is surprising the number of different ways there are to combine simple, traditional blocks.

My favorite part of the process, however, has always been the quilting. It is the "icing on the cake." I love designing the quilting motifs to fill the quieter spaces on the quilt's surface with texture. And I love the meditative nature of the actual quilting stitches, whether made by hand or by machine.

AWARDS:

AQS

Best Hand Workmanship

2003

Canyon Quilters of SAN DIEGO

Our purpose "is to promote good fellowship among persons interested in the art of quiltmaking and to promote the knowledge and appreciation of all aspects of quiltmaking."

Working on donation projects such as this one provides our members with a great sense of satisfaction.

POPPIES AND OTHER CALIFORNIA BEAUTIES
88" x 112", Canyon Quilters of San Diego, San Diego, CA, 1991. Cottons; hand appliquéd, hand embroidered, and hand quilted.
1992.20.01

ERIKA CARTER

A passion for creating something of substance from raw materials led me to quilting.

It is this same "making" that has helped me find the strength and resiliency to be found in what is sensitive and fragile. I want to portray the poetry in the visual.

These early works are an attempt to manage (I no longer want to use the word "control") chaos, as portrayed by my use of color.

FREEDOM'S CASCADE
44" x 66", Erika Carter, Bellevue, WA, 1990. Cottons; machine pieced, hand appliquéd, and hand quilted.
1997.06.24

ERIKA CARTER

GRACE
45" x 69", Erika Carter, Bellevue, WA, 1993. Hand painted and commercial cottons; machine appliquéd and machine quilted.
1997.07.11

ERIKA CARTER

SUBMERGENCE
71" x 53", Erika Carter, Bellevue, WA, 1989. Cottons; machine pieced, hand appliquéd, and hand quilted.
1997.06.79

MARY CHARTIER

Mary believes quiltmakers should make work that suits themselves. She personally does better technical work if she knows it will be judged, but choices of design, color, and fabric should be governed by the individual's preferences.

MORNING GLORY
80" x 100", Mary Chartier, New London, CT, 1986. Cottons; hand appliquéd, hand and machine pieced, and hand quilted.
1992.17.01

AWARDS:
Second Place
Appliqué, Professional
1988

HOLLIS CHATELAIN

"I had a friend in who lived in Yemen who had a beautiful book about the country," writes Hollis Chatelain. "I was intrigued with the photographs of the steps and terraces, and made a series of drawings from the photographs. I then turned those drawings into quilts with colors from my imagination. TERRACED LANDSCAPE is the largest quilt in the series."

Hollis Chatelain has continued to develop her artistic vision through quiltmaking. She has won numerous awards, including International Quilt Association Best of Show. Her quilt Sahel was named one of the Top 100 Quilts of the 20th Century. She has created Imagine Hope, an exhibition of her quilts and photographs by world famous photographers that strives to touch its viewers, inspiring them to get involved and make a change in the world.

TERRACED LANDSCAPE
85" x 39", Hollis Chatelain, Hillsborough, NC, 1995. Cotton fabrics, polyester batting; hand-dye-painted, machine pieced, machine quilted. 2011.07.01

NANCY CLARK

PHOENIX RISING
95½" x 80", Nancy Clark, Phoenix, AZ, 1987.
Cottons; machine pieced, hand appliquéd, hand painted, and hand quilted.
1997.06.56

Nancy's work has been inspired and informed by the intersection of childhood memories of the Arizona desert, dairy farming, veterinary medicine, and time spent in cities and suits.

JANE BURCH COCHRAN

DEVILED AND ANGEL

65" x 54", Jane Burch, Cochran, Rabbit Hash, KY, 2003. Thai silk, cottons, blends, recycled articles (gloves, net blouse, handkerchief, doily), beads, buttons, sequins, paint, color pencil, fortunes Xerox-transferred to fabric, Sulky rayon thread, Gutterman thread, cotton embroidery thread; machine pieced, hand appliquéd, hand embellished, machine quilted. 2010.10.01

This original design was inspired by two images I had used before but wanted to use again together. These images are the gloves forming wings and the deviled egg plate (a Southern tradition).

DEVILED AND ANGEL became my 9/11 quilt since I started working on it 9/11/2002, the one-year anniversary of that horrid day. The fortunes remind us what might have been for these many lives that were taken that day.

Collection of The National Quilt Museum

BARBARA L. CRANE

I hope my fabric landscapes suggest a sense of magic realism. I try to create surprise and predictability at the same time, to reflect my wonder and appreciation of the natural world. I often use hand-dyed and hand-painted fabrics to suggest sky and water, and to create illusions of light and shadow.

Transformation is a favorite magical tool: scraps of old plaid shirts turn into farmers' fields; pale calicoes resemble distant flower patches; batiks, cut just right, become snowy ridges, gnarled tree limbs, and birds' beaks.

Quilting lines are transformable, as well, into furrows, flight lines of birds, water currents, and the swirl of the wind. Meticulous hand quilting supports one of my personal goals—to find a place of stillness in myself.

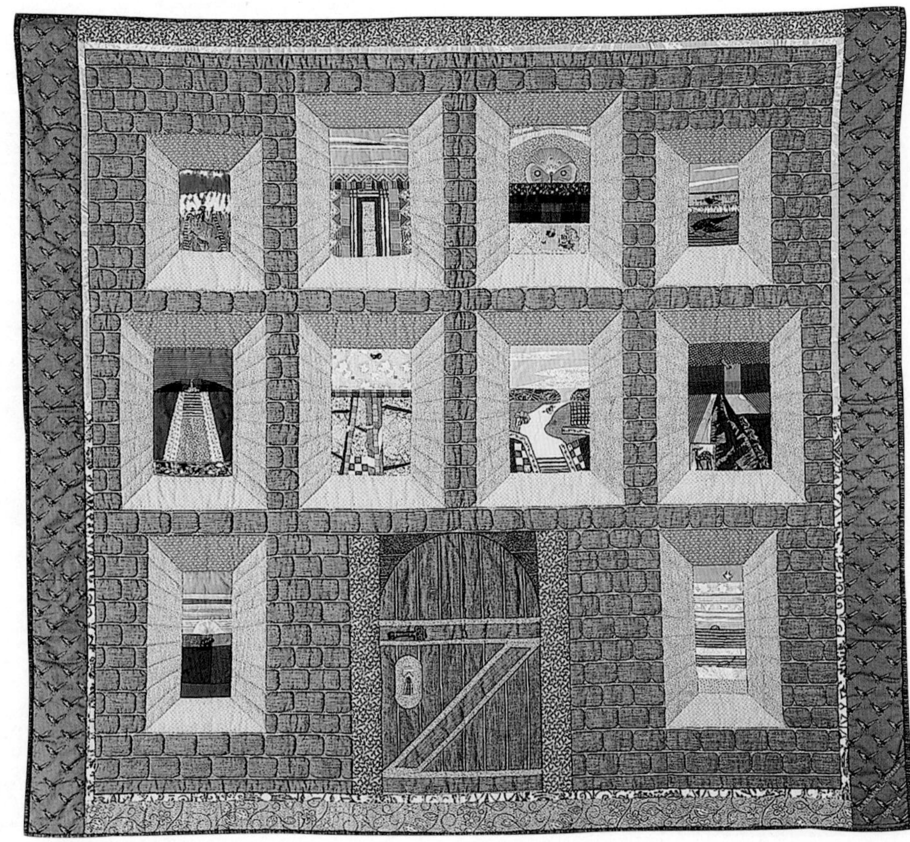

OUTLOOKS
58" x 51", Barbara L. Crane, Lexington, MA, 1984. Cottons and cotton blends; hand pieced, machine pieced, hand quilted, and embellished with small objects.
1997.06.53

AWARDS:

Third Place Wall Quilts, Amateur

1985

Lenore Crawford

AWARDS:
Moda
Best Wall Quilt
2011

Port of Cassis was created from a photo that I took in the south of France in the small port of Cassis at dusk. This piece took me nearly a year to finish because constructing a fused piece can sometimes be complicated. I left off the lower water part for several months until I figured out how I was going to construct it.

Fabric is an incredible flexible warm medium. The fabric helps to make it better than a photo and can actually add so much more depth than a painting on canvas.

Port of Cassis
52" x 48", Lenore Crawford, Midland, MI, 2010. Cottons, various and monofilament thread, fusing material, fabric paint, Warm & Natural™ cotton batting; machine pieced, painted, fused, raw-edge appliqué, machine quilted.
2011.03.03

Laura Crews-Lewis

Before she passed away, a love of paper dolls and learning to quilt early from her mother guided Laura's design and quilt-making efforts.

Up, Up, and Away
79" x 79", Laura Crews-Lewis, Cape Girardeau, MO, 1983. Cottons, chintz; hand appliquéd, hand quilted, stuffed, and Seminole pieced.
1997.06.89

MOLLY CULP

AUTUMN SERENADE
95" x 95", Molly Culp, Waco, TX, 2010. Cottons, Aurafil 50-weight thread, Hobbs 9 ounce poly batting for trapunto, Hobbs wool batting for quilt; machine pieced, machine appliqué, paper pieced, longarm machine quilted.
2011.03.04

Just before I retired in 1998, my husband bought me a Gammill longarm machine. I found my passion. I was determined to learn from each quilt I quilted so I could be the best quilter I could be.

I was inspired by the quality and detail of Sharon Schambers' workmanship. I enjoy being challenged and her work was a challenge to me. I especially admired Sharon's SCARLET SERENADE and decided to make my version of her quilt. I spent about three years making Autumn Serenade including just under 300 hours of quilting.

I used Sharon's machine appliqué method from the book *Piece by Piece Appliqué* which included soaking the quilt top in hot water for two hours. This made the tiny machine appliqué stitch look like hand appliqué.

AWARDS:
APQS Longarm Machine Quilting
2011

Judy Dales

The main portion of the design is pieced, and then additional layers of transparent fabric are applied to the background areas, creating a soft, diffuse effect similar to watercolor. A curved motif, repeated in a number of different ways, is reminiscent of blossoms, buds or flames. The red areas mingle with the blue, bringing to mind the merging of two elements as diverse as fire and water.

Fire on the Water
50¾" x 63¾", Judy Dales, Greensboro, VT, 2000. Cotton, chiffon, tulle, rayon and cotton thread, cotton batt; machine pieced, machine appliquéd, machine quilted.
2010.11.01

MARY JO DALRYMPLE

Aside from using up my pile of fabric and having done a lot of thinking while making quilts, I would hope that one achievement has been that others have shared my joy in the process.

ROCOCO ISLANDS
94" x 94", Mary Jo Dalrymple, Omaha, NE, 1982. Cottons; hand pieced and hand quilted.
1993.01.01

Francelise Dawkins

The creation of quilts using Francelise's "silkollage" technique involves layering silks, appliqué, painting, embroidery, and machine quilting. Exhibited and published nationally, she teaches her collage technique via lectures.

Discovery
18½" diameter, Francelise Dawkins, Queensbury, NY, 1991. Silks; machine appliquéd, machine embroidered, and machine quilted.
1997.07.07

Claudia Dawson

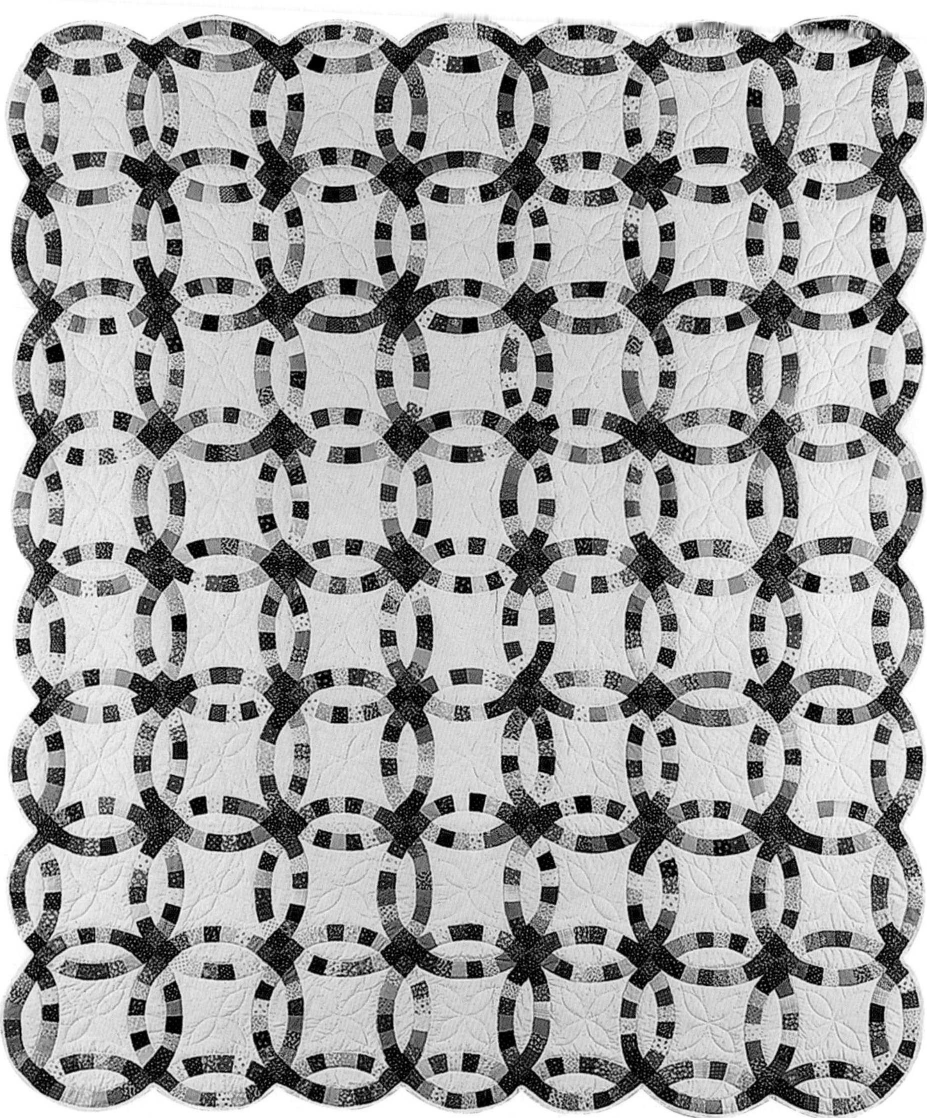

Quiltmaking for Claudia evolved from something she watched her mother do to a fulfilling pastime pursued while her husband was working away from home.

Double Wedding Ring
93" x 108", Claudia Dawson, Harviell, MO, 1985. Cottons, cotton polyester blends; machine pieced and hand quilted.
1997.06.18

Hanne Vibeke de Koning-Stapel

A pioneer quilting instructor in Holland, Hanne discovered quilting on a vacation in Vermont and learned how to quilt from Sophie Campbell in Paris.

Stella Antigua
91" x 91", Hanne Vibeke de Koning-Stapel, Bilthoven, Holland, 1988.
Silks; hand pieced and hand quilted.
1993.03.01

Awards:
First Place
Traditional Pieced, Professional
1989

Jo Diggs

Snow Scape
72" x 62", Jo Diggs, Portland, ME, c. 1995. Wools; machine pieced, hand appliquéd and quilted.
2004.02.01

Sewing and maintaining an avid interest in art have fueled the creativity in Jo's landscape quilts and her passion for teaching over several decades.

ADABELLE DREMANN

According to her son, the late Adabelle had more ideas than time when it came to putting her ideas into quilts, even though she stretched the days by quilting in kerosene lamp light.

AWARDS:
First Place
Pictorial Wall Quilt
1990

CORN CRIB
42" x 47", Adabelle Dremann, Princeton, IL, 1989. Cottons; machine pieced, hand appliquéd, hand embroidered, and hand quilted with trapunto.
1997.06.13

ADABELLE DREMANN

COUNTRY SCHOOL
73" x 92", Adabelle Dremann, Princeton, IL, 1988. Cottons; machine pieced, hand appliquéd, and hand quilted.
1992.01.01

AWARDS:
Second Place
Appliqué, Amateur
1989

Pat Durbin

Pat Durbin and her husband took a walk in Redwood Park in Arcata, California where Pat grew up to find a scene she could use in her work. "The walk was slow," Pat writes. "When I saw the stairway, inspiration hit! Usually I try to eliminate any 'man-made' elements in my pictures- but for some reason this stairway appealed to me. The sun was shining down the stairs and in this shot there was a weed or vine that showed itself to great advantage. When we came home and I viewed all of the shots- this was the one I decided to try."

Forest Walk
67" x 86", Pat Durbin, Eureka, CA, 2010. Cottons, nylon tulle, Superior thread, Sulky rayon thread, polyester Bottom Line thread by Superior, Hobbs Wool batting; machine pieced, raw edge appliquéd, machine quilted. 2010.13.01

Patricia EATON & Donna Fite McCONNELL

OUR SECRET GARDEN
87" x 87", Patricia Eaton and Donna Fite McConnell, Searcy, AR, 1990. Cottons; machine pieced, hand appliquéd, and hand quilted.
1997.06.52

Being the only person in my family who loved to sew, all I really wanted to do was learn to make a nice quilt. Eventually I did.

Then, I loved to share my ideas with those around me who made quilts, so I began to teach quiltmaking.

Now, many years later, I still teach a little. I just want to design and make my own quilts and the embroidered pieces I love, share them on my blog, and sometimes even sell a piece or two. It's fun and a great way to share what I love to do with people all over the planet.

I continue to learn and I'm still thrilled with the magic of what can be done with a needle and thread!

Patricia Eaton

Immersion in almost every aspect of the quilt industry has influenced Donna's approach to quiltmaking.

Donna Fite McConnell

ELLEN ANNE EDDY

"I've always loved the beauty of beetles," writes Ellen Anne Eddy. "Like every girl in America, I've grown up believing I could never be beautiful. I am convinced that we simply bash girl children into believing we are never good enough.

"Somewhere in there, my father brought me bits of nature. He brought water lilies, fish in jars, beetles and moths from his fishing trips; he took me in little boats. My bugs are a celebration of my own wild beauty and yours, past fashion, past convention. The beauty of individuation is a scary thing indeed. And lovely.

"DANCING IN THE LIGHT was done largely through new technique of using felt as a stabilizer for bobbin work images. I found I could do larger and more dramatic images."

DANCING IN THE LIGHT
55" x 69", Ellen Anne Eddy, Porter, IN, 2008. Hand-dyed cotton, lace, lamé, brocade, polyester thread, Candlelight thread, Razzle Dazzle thread, Glamoor thread, #5 pearl cotton, monofilament nylon thread, stabilizers, felt, Warm and Natural™ Batt; machine pieced, machine appliquéd, bobbin worked, digital threadwork designed by the artist, fused, machine quilted.
2010.09.01

Chris Wolf Edmonds

Inspiration for her artistry has come to Chris via the expanse of the prairie, devoid of visual distraction but abundant with color and texture.

Trees: Summer/Winter
41" x 51", Chris Wolf Edmonds, Lawrence, KS, 1999. Cotton, water-based pigments; hand painted and printed, machine pieced, and machine quilted. 2001.03.01

B. J. Elvgren

B. J.'s quilts are known for their pictorial qualities, to which she brings a folk-art perspective.

AWARDS:
First Place
Appliqué, Professional
1985

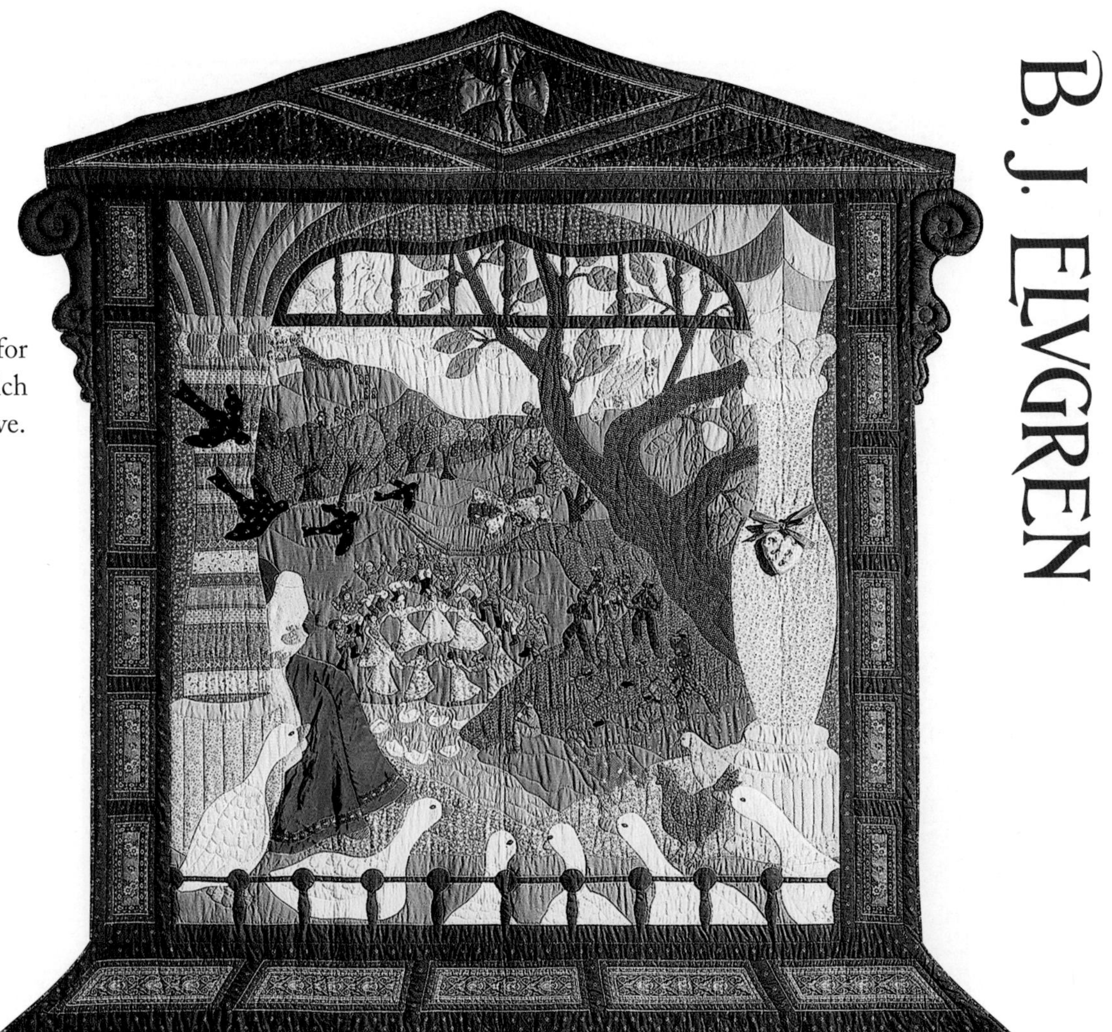

Twelve Days of Christmas
102" x 108", B. J. Elvgren, Chesapeake, VA, 1983. Cottons, velvets, and silks; hand appliquéd, hand quilted with trapunto, and hand embroidered.
1997.06.88

LINDA GOODMON EMERY

For Linda, the definition of achieving quilt artistry is to set high goals and pursue them persistently.

ROSEMALING INSPIRATION
81" x 95", Linda Goodmon Emery, Derby, KS, 1986. Cottons and flexible ribbon floss embellishment; hand appliquéd and hand quilted. National Quilting Association Masterpiece Quilt.
1997.06.65

AWARDS:
Second Place
Appliqué, Professional
1986

Jean M. EVANS & Joyce MURRIN

As a quiltmaker, I work with enthusiasm and patience, drawing from experiences and things imagined.

Inspiration comes from within and from the observation of color, light, line, form, texture, and pattern on faces, figures, ordinary things, and in nature.

I strive for a high level of technical skill in hand appliqué, reverse appliqué, hand quilting, machine piecing, machine quilting, embellishing, and painting.

Jean M. Evans

My greatest joy in quiltmaking is the challenge—met head on and accomplished.

Now I have the freedom to be creative, to think and design artistically, and in the end, to make quilts from my own designs that are complex yet visually uncomplicated; still challenging; sometimes surprising; and for many reasons, pleasing to me.

Joyce Murrin

MAY SHADOWS
60" x 60", Jean M. Evans, Medina, OH, and Joyce Murrin, Orient, NY, 1985. Cottons, cotton blends; hand appliquéd and hand quilted.
1997.06.39

Caryl Bryer Fallert

Birds of a Different Color
74" x 93", Caryl Bryer Fallert, Oswego, IL, 1999. Hand-dyed cottons; machine pieced and machine quilted.
2000.01.01

The focus of my work is on the qualities of color, line, and texture, which engage the spirit and emotions of the viewer, evoking a sense of mystery, excitement, or joy inspired by visual impressions, collected in my travels, in my everyday life, and in my imagination.

Illusions of movement, depth, and luminosity are common to most of my work.

My quilts are about seeing, experiencing, and imagining, rather than pictorial representation of any specific object or species. When recognizable objects appear, they represent the emotions and flights of fantasy evoked by those objects.

I intend for my quilts to be seen and enjoyed by others. It is my hope that they will lift the spirits and delight the eyes of those who see them.

AWARDS:
Hancock's of Paducah
Best of Show
2000

Collection of The National Quilt Museum

CARYL BRYER FALLERT

CORONA II: SOLAR ECLIPSE
76" x 94," Caryl Bryer Fallert, Oswego, IL, 1989. Hand-dyed fabrics; machine pieced and machine quilted. Named one of the 100 Best American Quilts of the 20th Century.
1996.01.07

AWARDS:
AQS
Best of Show
1989

CARYL BRYER FALLERT

MIGRATION #2
88" x 88", Caryl Bryer Fallert, Oswego, IL, 1995. Cottons; dye painted, hand dyed, machine pieced, machine appliquéd, and machine quilted.
1996.01.18

AWARDS:
AQS
Best of Show
1995

Caryl Bryer Fallert

Red Poppies
72" x 90", Caryl Bryer Fallert, Oswego, IL, 1983. Cottons; machine pieced and hand quilted.
1997.06.62

Caryl Bryer Fallert

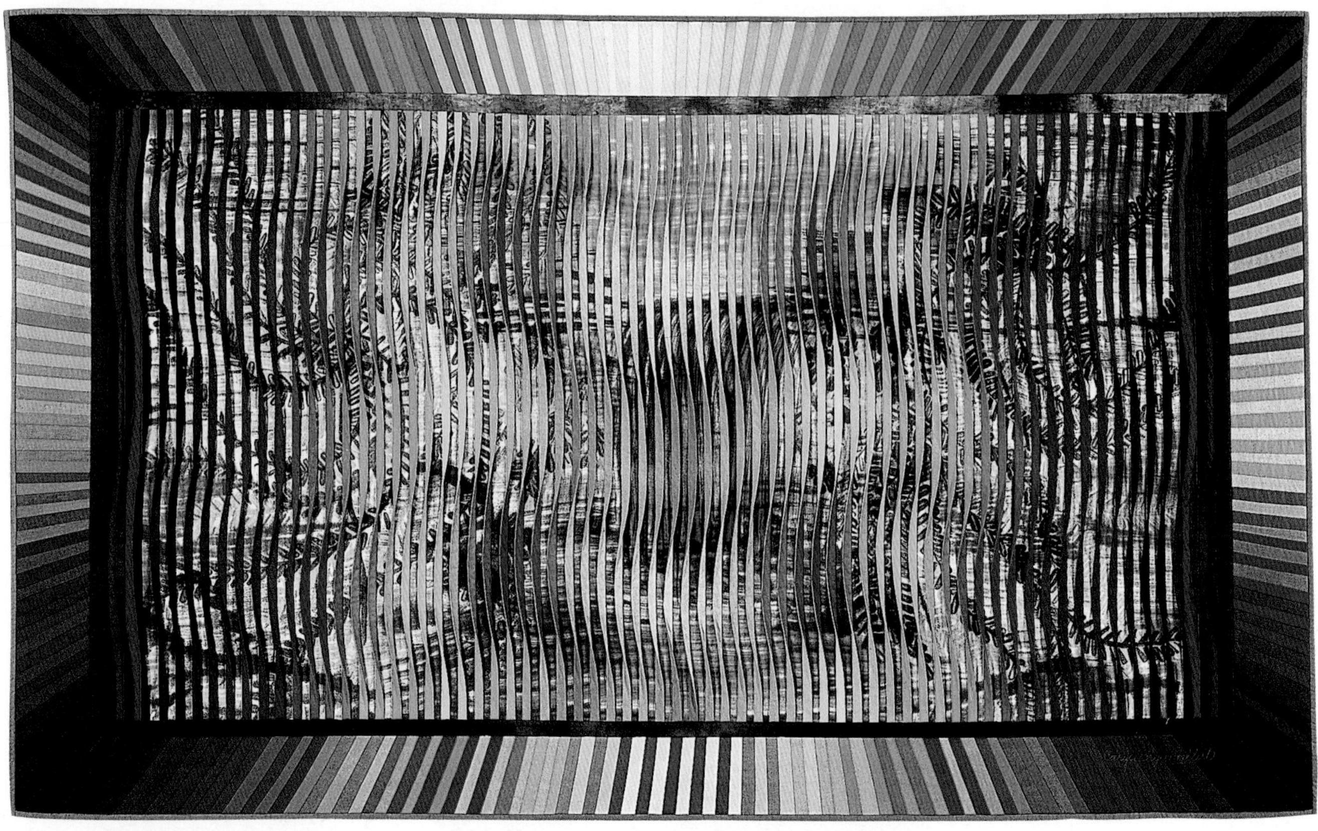

Reflection #3

77" x 45", Caryl Bryer Fallert, Oswego, IL, 1990. Hand-dyed, hand-painted fabrics; machine pieced and machine quilted.
1997.07.15

Hazel B. Reed Ferrell

I wanted to leave to the quilt world and my family footprints of my passing and knowledge of the arts illustrated in stitches.

I accomplished this by having three quilts with permanent homes in museums. One is in the Gerald R. Ford Museum in Grand Rapids, Michigan; one is in the History and Culture Center in Charleston, West Virginia; and one is in the [formerly] Museum of the American Quilter's Society in Paducah, Kentucky.

I am now 82 years old, very proud to have accomplished my mission, and to all of you out there for giving me the opportunity to achieve my goals, thank you.

Nature's Walk
99" x 103", Hazel B. Reed Ferrell, Middlebourne, WV, 1983. Cotton blends; hand appliquéd and hand quilted.
1997.06.41

DOROTHY FINLEY

DOT'S VINTAGE 1983
84" x 100", Dorothy Finley, Cordova, TN, 1983. Cottons; hand appliquéd and hand quilted with trapunto. National Quilting Association Masterpiece Quilt. 1996.01.10

One day Dorothy's husband came home with some quilt books belonging to one of his co-workers. He thought the quilts in the books were something else. To appease him, Dot, as she was known, began looking through one of them. She kept looking and looking and was amazed at what she saw. So she decided to make quilts.

Dot would never let anyone see what she was currently working on. That way, no one else would start working on that same pattern.

She loved genealogy and the old quilts, and that's what she wanted to do—pass on the old patterns and designs so people can know and love them as she did.

From a phone conversation with the late Dorothy Finley on 12/30/2008—Judy Schwender, TNQM Curator

AWARDS:
Gingher
Hand Workmanship Award
1985

Marianne Fons & Liz Porter

We have loved quiltmaking ever since we learned how in the 1970s. Our designs have always been geared for mainstream quilters and presented to them through our books; our magazine, *Love of Quilting;* and our television programs on public TV.

Often inspired by the works of anonymous nineteenth- and early twentieth- century American quilters, we enjoy simplifying and updating basic techniques in order to make projects easy and accessible for today's hobby quilters.

Stars & Stripes
80" x 96", Marianne Fons and Liz Porter, Winterset, IA, 2001.
Machine pieced; machine quilted by Jean Nolte.
2007.04.01

GAIL GARBER

AZIMUTH
110" x 110", Gail Garber, Albuquerque, NM, 1989. Cottons; hand pieced, hand quilted.
2013.03.01

"My earliest quilts are in the traditional style with conservative fabric choices," writes Gail Garber. "However, by 1984, I began to explore original design, after being inspired by the quilts of Jinny Beyer. My first effort, AZIMUTH, is a king-size medallion style quilt that features a Mariner's Compass in the center and variations of the compass throughout the quilt. Still a traditionalist, the quilt was entirely hand-stitched and quilted from 1984-1989.

"This was my first original design. I joined a work study group to learn medallion style drafting, taught by Ruby Chick, who was in her 80s at the time."

Gail Garber

"Cosmic Parade was the second quilt in the style for which I have become known," writes Gail Garber. "In this quilt, I wanted the stars to be static, like the floats in a parade. The largest star in the lower-right corner represents the light of a rising star with others more distant in the background. Typical of many of my more recent quilts, the fractured background features tone-on-tone flying geese that add subtle motion and detail. This was the first time I had ever rounded a corner on a quilt—that was quite liberating. Now many of my quilts lack corners."

Cosmic Parade
50" x 67", Gail Garber, Albuquerque, NM, 2001. Cottons, 80/20 cotton/poly batt, monofilament nylon thread, Sulky Sliver Opalescent thread; machine pieced, machine quilted.
2013.03.02

Donna Duchesne GAROFALO

Donna combined love of family, painting, and sewing into a lucrative, expressive quilting practice.

SERENITY II: LIFE IN MY POND
42" x 57", Donna Duchesne Garofalo, North Windham, CT, 1985. Cottons, cotton blends; machine pieced, hand quilted, and hand appliquéd.
1997.06.69

DIANE GAUDYNSKI

My vision is to create traditional quilts that transcend method, resulting in quilts with beautiful, interesting visual design, dimension, and purpose.

I work within a defined framework of tradition using a muted, sophisticated color palette, creating a fresh perspective from a modern vantage point.

My quilts are designed as I see them in my mind's eye; they are the quilts of today, using today's tools, a "new" tradition, but honoring and reflecting quilts of the past.

Quilting on my home sewing machine, I move the quilt under a carefully controlled needle to get precision, delicacy, and pleasing flow. I consider machine quilting fine needlework that refines and reflects the art and beauty of quilting as part of a long history of decorative arts.

AWARDS:

Bernina

Machine Workmanship

1999

BUTTERNUT SUMMER

81" x 81", Diane Gaudynski, Pewaukee, WI, 1998. Cottons; machine pieced and machine quilted.

1999.02.01

Diane Gaudynski

Kettle Moraine Star
91" x 91", Diane Gaudynski, Pewaukee, WI, 1996. Cottons; machine pieced and machine quilted.
1997.02.01

Awards:
Bernina
Machine Workmanship
1997

Diane Gaudynski

October Morning
82" x 82", Diane Gaudynski, Pewaukee, WI, 1999. Cottons; machine pieced, machine quilted with trapunto, and machine broderie perse.
2000.03.01

AWARDS:
Bernina
Machine Workmanship
2000

Diane Gaudynski

Shadows of Umbria
83" x 83", Diane Gaudynski, Waukesha, WI, 2006. Cottons, silk dupioni; machine pieced and quilted.
2008.05.01

Awards:
Bernina
Machine Workmanship
2008

DIANE GAUDYNSKI

SWEETHEART ON PARADE
83" x 83", Diane Gaudynski, Pewaukee, WI, 1997. Cottons; machine pieced and machine quilted.
1998.03.01

AWARDS:
Bernina
Machine Workmanship
1998

CANDY GOFF

JOIE DE VIE – JOY OF LIFE
94" x 94", Candy Goff, Lolo, MT, 1998. Cottons; hand pieced, hand appliquéd, and hand quilted. Named one of the 100 Best American Quilts of the 20th Century.
1999.01.01

I hope to achieve a connection to the history and tradition of quiltmaking.

Today's cutting-edge quilts have examples of techniques used in antique quilts that we now perceive as innovative.

I often use antique quilts as inspiration to make an original design. To keep the traditional style of quiltmaking a viable art, I think it's important to maintain the creativity that was prevalent in early quilts. No two were the same.

My quilts are done entirely "by hand." This allows many hours of creative decision making as the design progresses. I enjoy the tactile feel of the fabric and quilt sandwich in my hands as the quilt nears completion.

I hope to continue the traditional quilt as an art form for the future.

AWARDS:
Hancock's of Paducah
Best of Show
1999

MARY GOLDEN

Family quilts nurtured my early love of quilts. They were windows into the lives of my mother's family and perpetuated this wonderful tradition.

Quilts speak volumes about their makers' lives, as my quilts have been reflective of 36 years of my life changes.

Through designs, fabrics, and colors, my enthusiasm and encouragement for all quilters and their talents remain constant.

With my quilts—created for physical and emotional warmth, for self, gift, or purchase—the teaching of techniques, the enjoyment of the sewing process, and the promotion of bonds between quilters are the most important elements of my quiltmaking.

NE'ER ENCOUNTER PAIN
90" x 90", Mary Golden, Gloucester, MA, 1982. Cottons; hand pieced and hand quilted.
1997.06.42

IMOGENE GOOCH

I have two quilts in museums and at my age I would just like to finish the quilts I have started.

I will always quilt, however; I think it's in my blood.

I am so thankful for my mother making me help her do the quilting. Every winter she would have one [quilt] in the frame. I have acquired some 1930-40 quilt tops, so I have been working on them.

FEATHERED STAR SAMPLER
97" x 97", Imogene Gooch, Rockville, IN, 1983. Cottons; hand pieced and hand quilted.
1997.06.21

AWARDS:
Second Place
Patchwork, Professional
1985

Irene Goodrich

What I hope to achieve with the artistry of my quiltmaking is difficult for me to answer as I'm in my eighties and a much better quilter than a writer!

To me quilting is a soothing, rewarding therapeutic experience. Beginning in 1970 I was a caregiver for several family members. During all the difficult times, prayers and quilting kept me sane. So to you quilters out there, should you find yourself in the same situation, keep on quilting!

I feel that quilting has helped me reach my older age and it is my hope that I will be able to add many more years to my age with my love of quilting.

Lancaster County Rose
90" x 110", Irene Goodrich, Columbus, OH, 1980. Cottons and cotton blends; hand pieced and hand quilted.
1997.06.31

ALISON GOSS

ANCIENT DIRECTIONS
80" x 67," Alison Goss, Durango, CO, 1991. Cottons; machine pieced and machine quilted. Named one of the 100 Best American Quilts of the 20th Century.
1996.01.02

My art emerges from my meditation practices and reflects my desire to explore the mystery of consciousness—that field of awareness that permeates and gives meaning to the universe.

My work explores those edges where science and spirituality come together as I play with my understanding in both quantum physics and spiritual inquiry, knowing that they both point to the same truth of oneness.

I create as a meditative practice, opening to the stillness in each moment, engaging the intelligence of my heart, becoming one with the flow of creativity.

This practice strengthens my ability to experience the beauty of deep presence in every moment of my life, to move with grace through difficult times, and to help others do the same.

AWARDS:

RJR

Best Wall Quilt

1991

Alison Goss

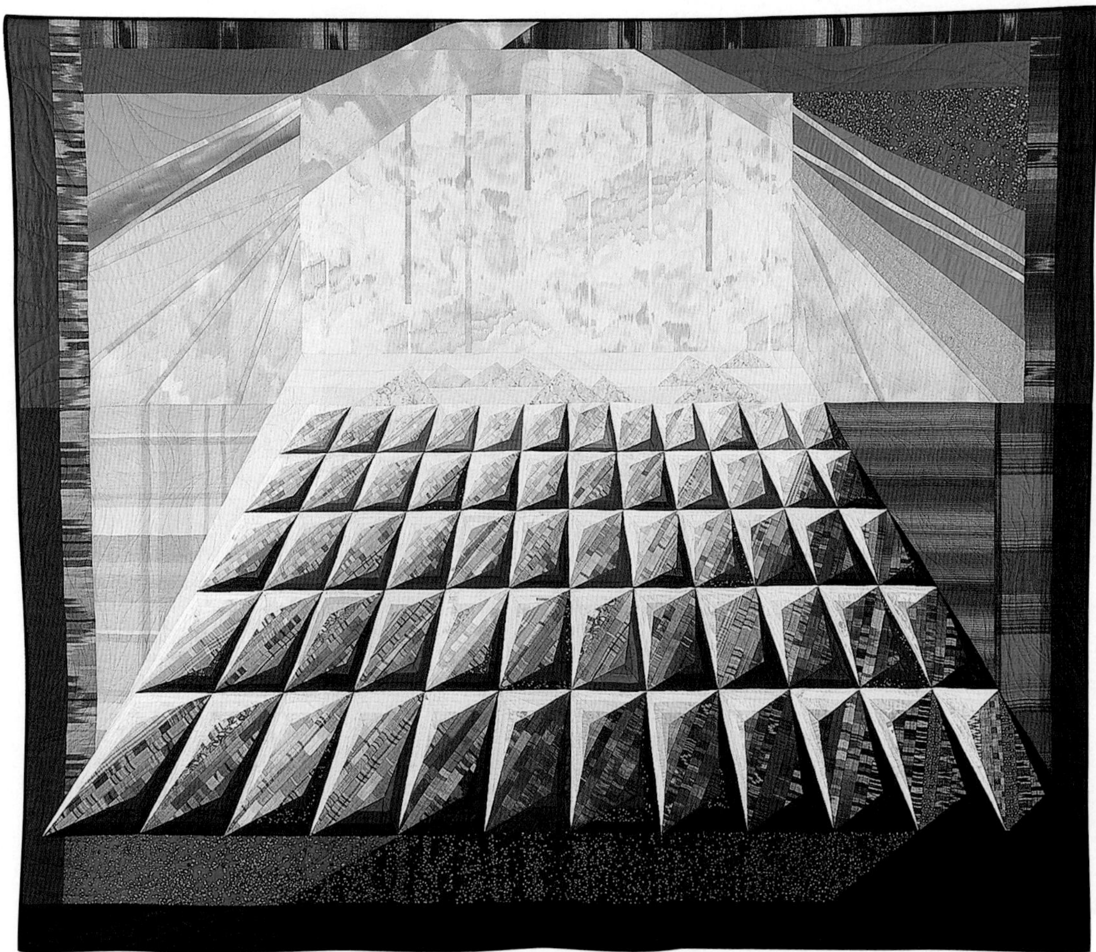

Restoring the Balance
95" x 80", Alison Goss, Durango, CO, 1990. Cottons and poly-cotton blends; machine pieced and hand quilted.
1992.08.01

MARY L. HACKETT

I hope to convince all of my students and readers that there is no limit to what they can make with fabric.

All that is required is an inspiration, a desire, and an open-minded, inquisitive approach to techniques one has not tried.

Excitement, pleasure, and satisfaction await the person willing to try a new method, practice it, and apply it in a new way to his or her ideas.

FEAR OF THE DARK
87" x 87", Mary L. Hackett, Carterville, IL, 1993. Cottons; machine pieced and machine quilted.
1997.07.10

Renae HADDADIN & Karen Kay BUCKLEY

Colorful pottery and tile designs Karen saw while often vacationing in Mexico were her inspiration. Although proficient on a computer, Karen says it is difficult for her to envision how the finished product will appear from a 3" image on a screen so she sticks with her tried-and-true system of sketching each individual panel to size with pencil and paper until she is satisfied with the results. After completing the top, Karen shipped it from her home in Pennsylvania to Renae in Utah.

Renae says when she received the quilt top, she "just looked at it for a while" before beginning the quilting on her Innova longarm. She carefully decided on varying designs for each individual section.

The quilt top took Karen a year to design and appliqué and Renae an additional year to quilt.

AWARDS:

Janome of America

Best of Show

2013

FIESTA MEXICO

85" x 90", Renae Haddadin and Karen Kay Buckley, Sandy UT, 2012. Cottons; machine pieced, hand appliquéd, longarm machine quilted.

2013.06.01

JANE HALL

PINEAPPLE LOG CABIN
50" x 68", Jane Hall, Raleigh, NC, 1985. Cottons; machine pieced and hand quilted.
1997.06.57

I hope to make quilts in the best tradition of the quiltmaker's art. I want the colors and the design to "sing," both for me and for the viewer. My quilts are most often fabric or color inspired, although sometimes I am influenced by the designs in antique quilts.

I enjoy exploring traditional patterns, especially in the Log Cabin/Pineapple family, with contemporary coloration and innovative tweaks and an occasional element of unpredictability.

The entire process of planning, designing, and constructing the quilt has a twofold meaning for me: it is a wonderfully satisfying tactile art form, and, at the same time, I have the sense of following in our foremothers' footsteps, making *woman's art.*

VICKIE HALLMARK

Following my training and practice as a research scientist, my approach to quilting is decidedly experimental.

As scientists seek for truth and understanding in small, well-defined inquiries, quilters may piece together bits and pieces into an artistic theory of life.

My quilts are autobiographical in that real life issues are always represented in the overriding themes of the work, although it may not be recognizable to anyone other than myself. Indeed, the generation of real life solutions seems intimately connected to resolutions of artistic and technical problems during the art process.

As I work, I disassemble a problem and reassemble a solution, both in the quilt and in life. The name of any piece can immediately pinpoint a date, location, and concern in my memory.

AWARDS:

Bernina
Machine Workmanship
2001

ENLIGHTENMENT
85" x 85", Vicki Hallmark, Austin, TX, 2000. Cottons; polyester and metallic threads; machine pieced, machine appliquéd, and machine quilted.
2001.11.01

MIYUKI HAMABA

WITH YOU

86" x 86", Miyuki Hamaba, Sanda, Hyogo, Japan, 2009. Cotton, sateen, embroidery thread; hand appliquéd, hand pieced, hand embroidered, hand quilted.
2011.03.06

Miyuki Hamaba has been making quilts for about 20 years and says quilting is the spice that adds excitement and pleasure to her life. Now an advanced quilting instructor with the Japan Handi Crafts Instructors' Association, she usually enjoys hand piecework and quilting, and doesn't do appliqué very often. The inspiration for her stunningly beautiful Baltimore Album style quilt was one she saw at an exhibition about ten years ago. That quilt prompted her to change her norm and appliqué one for herself. WITH YOU was two and a half years in the making.

For her quilt, Miyuki humbly explains, "There is nothing special about my appliqué. I just keep every piece's seam allowance to three millimeters, fold it, and sew; that is all. Appliqué needs careful and refined work."

AWARDS:

AQS

Hand Workmanship

2011

Cindy Vermillion HAMILTON

My reasons, methods, and interests in making quilts have changed little since the 1960s, when I was swept into the fascinating world of creating beautiful quilts.

As a history lover, I enjoy mentally traveling to times past as I hand stitch classic patterns, colors, and fabric styles into new arrangements that lift my spirit and make my soul sing.

I build my quilts upon recognizable elements and motifs that women of the past created. This allows me to be part of the wide world of female energy and imagery that has been captured and lovingly passed down to us through stitches.

I hope my quilts inspire others to be part of this journey that captures time.

OLDE ENGLISH MEDALLION
104" x 104", Cindy Vermillion Hamilton, Pagosa Springs, CO, 1992. Cottons; hand pieced, hand appliquéd, and hand quilted.
1992.22.01

AWARDS:
First Place
Traditional Pieced, Professional
1992

GLORIA HANSEN

BLUSHING TRIANGLES 3
41½" x 42", Gloria Hansen, East Windsor, NJ, 2008. Original digital painting; printed, painted, machine pieced and quilted.
2008.06.01

My goal is to merge my love of creating art using digital media with my love of quiltmaking to create work that pays respect to tradition while pushing its boundaries into tomorrow's possibilities.

I hope my quilt art first grabs the attention of the viewer and then draws the viewer in, evoking a sense of wonder.

Rather than the viewer being intrigued with the how, I'd rather the viewer enjoy the visual experience and contemplate the why.

AWARDS:
Moda
Best Wall Quilt
2008

IRMA GAIL HATCHER

Hand workmanship, three-dimensional applique, and a love of flowers are the foundations of Irma Gail's artistry and achievements.

AWARDS:
Gingher
Hand Workmanship
1994

CONWAY ALBUM (I'M NOT FROM BALTIMORE)
86" x 89", Irma Gail Hatcher, Conway, AR, 1992. Cottons; hand appliquéd and hand quilted. Named one of the 100 Best American Quilts of the 20th Century and a National Quilting Association Masterpiece Quilt.
1996.01.06

IRMA GAIL HATCHER

GARDEN MAZE
82" x 82", Irma Gail Hatcher, Conway, AR, 1998. Cottons; machine pieced, hand appliquéd, and hand quilted with trapunto.
2000.02.01

AWARDS:
Timeless Treasures
Hand Workmanship
2000

DENISE TALLON HAVLAN

Seeing Amish quilts and falling in love with them, I entered the world of quiltmaking with very little sewing experience but a great willingness to learn.

In time I moved into the "art quilt" arena and let my imagination go. My intentions and goals are always directed toward creating one-of-a-kind images that portray the natural world and the people who inhabit it.

My ultimate purpose is to be part of leaving a legacy of how the beautiful and purposeful craft of quiltmaking continues to evolve with each generation's vision. Whether using traditional designs handed down from our ancestors or discovering new paths untraveled, we are keeping the art of the quilt alive forever!

AWARDS:
2nd Place
AQS Quilt Exposition,
Nashville, Tennessee
2000

MUSES FOR A MILLENNIUM
72" x 80", Denise Tallon Havlan, Plainfield, IL, 2000. Cotton and synthetic commercial fabrics, textile paints and inks, Prismacolor® pencils; cotton, rayon, and metallic threads; hand and machine appliqué, fused; embellished, machine quilted.
2007.12.01

LAURA HEINE

ONE FISH, TWO FISH, RED FISH, BLUE FISH
82" x 92", Laura Heine, Billings, MT, 1993. Cottons; machine pieced and machine quilted.
1996.01.21

I have been teaching and quilting professionally for more than 15 years and have developed a deep love and fascination with color and texture.

In quilting, it is the creative process that fascinates me, from concept through execution. I love the texture of the medium and the ability to express my artistic ideas through every step of the quilting process.

I am inspired by each aspect, from designing the fabrics, threads, and patterns on through the free-motion surface embellishment, quilting, and overquilting elements.

It is my hope that my artistic expression through quilting will serve as inspiration for new quilters to discover their own talent hidden inside and to develop their own sensational style!

AWARDS:
Bernina
Machine Workmanship
1994

MARILYN HENRION

I use color, line, and form much as a poet employs words to convey a particular emotion or idea.

As in poetry, the metaphorical images are meant to resonate, being both themselves and something they may suggest to the viewer. The works transcend the impersonal objectivity of geometric abstraction through the sensuousness of materials of which they are constructed, revealing a blend of reason and passion.

Paying homage to traditional techniques of hand piecing and hand quilting, my goal is to transform these materials into expressive works of art.

HERE BETWEEN
40½" x 40½", Marilyn Henrion, New York, NY, 1992. Cottons; machine pieced and hand quilted.
1997.07.12

VALETA HENSLEY

FASHIONABLE LADIES OF THE '20S
59½" x 61½", Valeta Hensley, Flemington, MO, 2009. Cottons, tapestry fabric; YLI silk thread, DMC 50wt cotton; machine embroidery thread, DMC embroidery floss; Hobbs Thermore polyester batt; hand appliquéd, hand assembled, longarm machine quilted by Bill "Quilting Bill" Fullerton.
2010.06.01

AWARDS:
Moda Best Wall Quilt
2010

"Inspiration for this quilt came from my love of 1920s fashions, challenging myself to use needleturn appliqué to make faces that look life-like, and a fondness for triptych designs," writes Valeta Hensley. She had never tried a three-panel design before attempting this quilt.

BECKY HERDLE

Experience judging at all levels, writing, teaching, and completing antique tops and blocks provide inspiration for Becky's own quiltmaking.

INDIAN BARN RAISING
86" x 96", Becky Herdle, Rochester, NY, 1988. Cottons; machine pieced and hand quilted.
2001.14.01

Ethel Hickman

Like so many quilters, Ethel's involvement in quilting has been in phases and has been influenced by the work of others as well as her own innate sense of color and style.

Ann Orr's "Ye Olde Sampler"
80" x 100", Ethel Hickman, Camden, AR, 1985. Poly/cotton blends, cottons; hand appliquéd, hand quilted with corded edge.
1997.06.02

Chizuko Hana Hill

A deep appreciation for beauty and workmanship guides Chizuko's quiltmaking.

Great American Elk
65" x 70", Chizuko Hana Hill, Garland, TX, 1994. Cottons; machine and hand pieced, hand quilted.
1998.05.01

MARY KAY HITCHNER

TULIPS AGLOW
54½" x 54½", Mary Kay Hitchner, Haverford, PA, 1989. Cottons; machine pieced and hand quilted.
1996.01.28

I push myself to develop or learn something new with every quilt.

AWARDS:
RJR
Best Wall Quilt
1990

Pat Holly

Designing and constructing PAISLEY PEACOCK took a little over a year. I do all my own designing and love looking at textiles from all over the world for ideas. The idea for the center of this quilt came from a picture I saw of a chintz fabric from India that had a peacock turning into a paisley. The outer borders were inspired by an exhibit I saw at the Burrell Collection outside of Glasgow, Scotland.

All the elements in the quilt were drawn first on tracing paper as I need to trace the fusible for the appliqué in reverse. The quilt is completely machine appliquéd; there is no piecing. The areas are appliquéd together with joining frames. I have mainly been making miniature quilts recently and this was my first larger quilt in a while. I wanted to make a piece that had more to it, although many of the elements are small scale.

AWARDS:

Janome Best of Show

2011

PAISLEY PEACOCK
60" x 72", Pat Holly, Ann Arbor, MI, 2009. Cotton, silk; Polyester, rayon, cotton, and silk threads; commercial trims; cotton/silk batt; machine appliquéd, machine quilted.
2011.03.01

Pat HOLLY & Sue NICKELS

THE BEATLES QUILT
95" x 95", Pat Holly, Muskegon, MI, and Sue Nickels, Ann Arbor, MI, 1998. Cottons; machine appliquéd, machine pieced, and machine quilted.
1998.01.01

AWARDS:
AQS
Best of Show
1998

My quilts are a culmination of a lifelong exposure [to quilts] and sewing, and my love of history and need to create. Old textiles from all over the world are an endless source of inspiration and wonder.

Art school skills and years of experience with the sewing machine allow me to design and produce quilts that satisfy my desire to pay tribute to textile creators of the past.

Pat Holly

My personal goal in quilting is to continue to make machine-made quilts that are inspired by the traditions in quilting.

Traveling and teaching inspire my quilts, too.

I want to push myself to be as creative as possible and use the sewing machine to create my work.

Sue Nickels

Pat HOLLY & Sue NICKELS

THE SPACE QUILT
87" x 87", Sue Nickels, Ann Arbor, MI, and Pat Holly, Muskegon, MI, 2004. Cottons; polyester and metallic threads; machine pieced, machine appliquéd, and machine quilted.
2004.01.02

AWARDS:
Bernina
Machine Workmanship
2004

Pamela Humphries

For me, quiltmaking is a perfect blending of the old and the new. I like to create fresh designs, then make the quilt the old-fashioned way—by hand.

With each quilt I hope to craft a piece that is visually appealing and constructed with top quality workmanship. Since I quilt purely for my own enjoyment, as long as I am pleased with the finished piece, then I have achieved my goal.

Feathered Beauties
70" x 83", Pamela Humphries, Larkspur, CO, 2005. Cottons, cotton and silk threads; hand pieced, appliquéd, and quilted.
2006.04.01

Awards:
AQS
Hand Workmanship
2006

MARION HUYCK

Letting the fabric speak and using it in new ways are at the core of Marion's quiltmaking.

TERRARIUM
40" x 50½", Marion Huyck, Chicago, IL, 1983. Cottons; hand pieced, machine pieced, hand appliquéd, reverse appliquéd, and hand quilted and embroidered.
1997.06.82

MARION HUYCK

AWARDS:
First Place – Wall Quilt, Professional
1986

NOTHING GOLD CAN STAY
71" x 57", Marion Huyck, Chicago, IL, 1985. Cottons; hand pieced, machine pieced, hand appliquéd, reverse appliquéd, and hand quilted.
1997.06.48

Lois K. Ide

My mother taught me to sew on an old treadle Singer when I was only four years old. I am now 88 years old, still sewing and quilting, writing, and teaching occasionally. Mama also taught me to share my talents.

What could be more rewarding than designing and making and being asked to share my quilts in churches, at school, and in other meetings as well as in quilt shows?

Now I am making numerous crazy quilts from all the bushels of scraps I have saved through the years.

Galaxy of Quilters
87" x 107", Lois K. Ide, Bucyrus, OH, 1983. Cottons and cotton blends; hand appliquéd, hand embroidered, machine pieced, and hand quilted.
1997.06.25

Collection of The National Quilt Museum

KATHERINE INMAN

Although she only creates quilts of her own design, Katherine believes that the efforts of other quilt artists should be appreciated.

ORIENTAL FANTASY
82" x 98", Katherine Inman, Athens, OH, 1984. Cottons; machine pieced, hand appliquéd, hand embroidered, and hand quilted.
1996.01.22

AWARDS:
AQS
Best of Show
1985

MICHAEL JAMES

ALETSCH
81" x 41", Michael James, Somerset Village, MA, 1990. Cottons, silk; machine pieced and machine quilted.
1997.06.01

One of my objectives is to challenge the notion of what quilts can be.

I want my imagery to point the viewer toward a deeper kind of looking, to provoke reflection, and perhaps to break down presumptions about what art is for.

Carolyn JOHNSON & Wilma JOHNSON

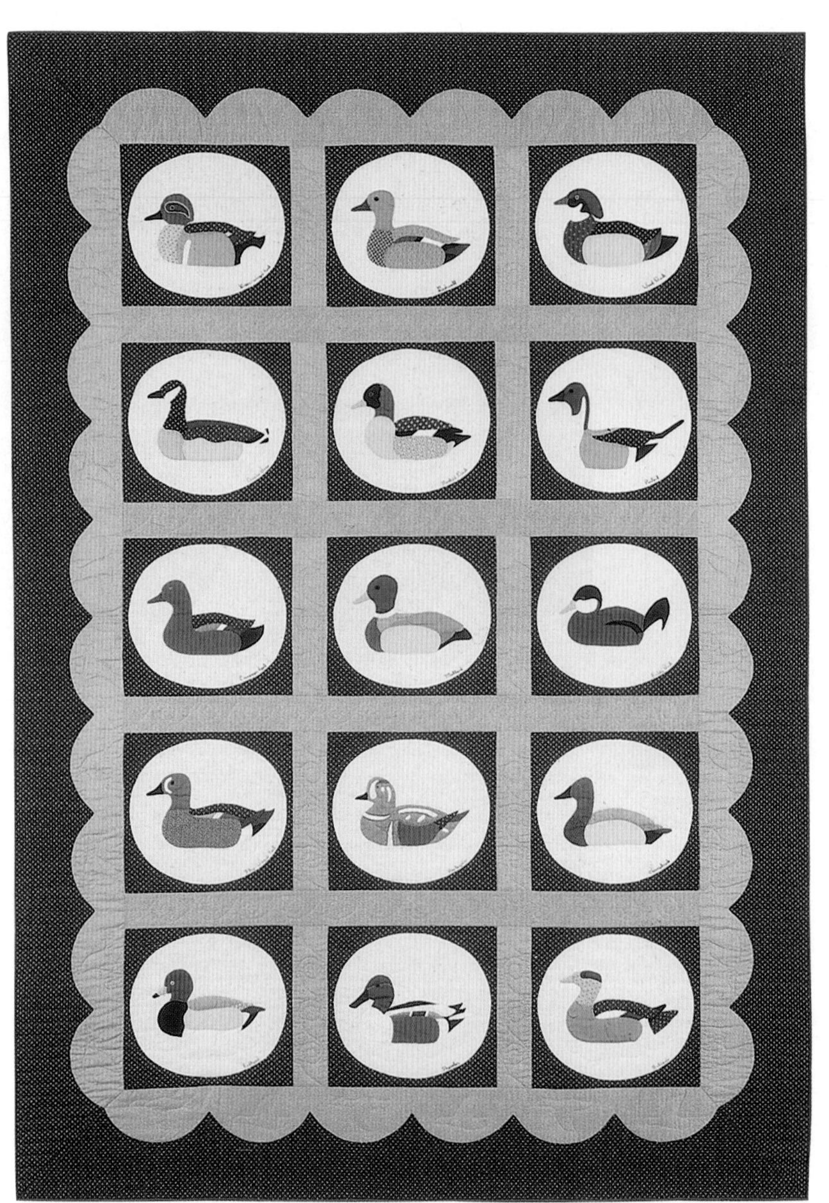

Creating quilts for their families gave sisters-in-law Carolyn and Wilma the opportunity to produce and sell art of their own design. FEATHERED FRIENDS was the first quilt acquired in the collection.

FEATHERED FRIENDS
63" x 91", Carolyn Johnson and Wilma Johnson, Symsonia, KY, 1984.
Cottons; hand appliquéd and hand quilted.
1997.06.20

MELODY JOHNSON

Quiltmaking should be fun; if it isn't, why do it?

I'm not out to prove I can achieve some sort of perfection. I want to have a great time making a quilt and have it look like fun when it is finished.

I believe that the design is paramount to the technique, and whatever it takes to create that piece is the right way to do it. I'm making art for the wall, not a functional bed quilt.

I choose to fuse so I can be expressive with fabric in ways that would be impossible with any other construction method. Scissors are a drawing tool; unfinished edges add character.

I especially enjoy improvising, but often find myself making up a design found in my sketchbook.

AWARDS:

RJR

Best Wall Quilt

1995

HOT FUN

56" x 63," Melody Johnson, Cary, IL, 1995. Hand-dyed cottons; machine embroidered, fused, and machine quilted.

1996.01.14

VICKI L. JOHNSON

My intent is to create something of beauty.

Using the California coastal area and other sites I experience as inspiration, my quilts reflect a love of nature. In combining painting with fabric techniques, I am working toward a rich surface. The texture of the commercial fabrics enhances the colors and painterly textures of the painting.

Adding quilting gives the work a relief structure with line work, like drawing over the color. The play of the quilting lines against both the piecing and painting adds an exciting visual element and suggests other layers of meaning. It also adds depth, like a relief sculpture.

If the viewer looks deeper than the surface richness, the elements used can be interpreted with symbology from several cultures that revere nature.

NIGHT BEACONS III
48" x 67", Vicki L. Johnson, Soquel, CA, 1991. Cottons; painted and machine appliquéd, machine and hand quilted.
1992.12.01

ANGELA W. KAMEN

The confluence of geometry, fabrics, and original design are at the core of Angela's artistic expression through quilts.

JELLY BEAN

57" x 77", Angela W. Kamen, Bedford Corners, NY, 1998. Cottons and silk organza; machine pieced, machine quilted, machine embroidered and couched.
1998.02.01

AWARDS:

RJR
Best Wall Quilt
1998

MARGIE T. KARAVITIS

A love of hand quilting sustained Margie's interest in quiltmaking throughout her lifetime.

CHERRY ROSE
95" x 94", Margie T. Karavitis, Spokane, WA, 1990. Cottons; hand appliquéd, hand and machine pieced, and hand quilted.
1992.13.01

MARGIE T. KARAVITIS

OH MY STARS
97" x 97", Margie T. Karavitis, Spokane, WA, 1989. Cottons; hand and machine pieced and hand quilted.
1992.15.01

AWARDS:
First Place
Traditional Pieced, Professional
1990

Bonnie Keller

Organic Garden
86½" x 86½", Bonnie Keller, Chehalis, WA, 2006. Cottons, silk and cotton threads, Ultrasuede® embroidery floss, Pigma® pens, acrylic yarn, Tsukineko® all-purpose ink; hand appliquéd, machine pieced, hand quilted.
2007.08.01

I set personal goals for myself that keep stretching me beyond what I've done in the past.

I always keep open to new insights as I work and ask myself, "what if."

I don't very often have my quilts planned from start to finish. Many times I end up interjecting elements found around me in nature. I love to put little animals, birds, or insects on my quilts.

Ultimately, I quilt to please myself. I love owning beautiful, well-made things.

Awards:
AQS Hand Workmanship
2007

SHIRLEY P. KELLY

FLOWERS OF THE CROWN
78½" x 58", Shirley P. Kelly, Colden, NY, 2002. Cottons, lamé, cotton and rayon threads; hand appliquéd, machine quilted. National Quilting Association Masterpiece Quilt. 2007.10.01

AWARDS:
First Place
Pictorial Wall Quilt
2003

As an art student, I was encouraged to depict two-dimensional objects in an abstract or non-representational manner. But I always liked the challenge of realism, especially the unique utilitarian forms and shapes of animals.

My first time at an AQS show, the realistic depictions in the pictorial quilt categories inspired me to develop a prepared-edge applique technique, which I have used now for about twenty years.

The personalities of the animals or birds that inhabit my quilts appeal to children and adults alike. Over and over again they tell me that these quilts make them smile. That is the ultimate justification for my work.

SHIRLEY P. KELLY

PANDAS 'ROUND THE WORLD
75" x 99", Shirley P. Kelly, Colden, NY, 1993. Cottons; hand appliquéd, machine pieced, and machine quilted. 1997.07.14

AWARDS:
Second Place
Amateur, Appliqué
1994

SHRILEY P. KELLY

PUFFINS

78" x 71", Shirley P. Kelly, Colden, NY, 2004. Cottons; hand appliquéd, machine quilted.
2005.01.02

AWARDS:
Bernina
Machine Workmanship
2005

SHIRLEY P. KELLY

AWARDS:
First Place, Large Wall Quilt, Home Sewing Machine Quilted
2010

During a trip to the Pueblo region of Arizona and New Mexico about 25 years ago, I discovered a book on Hopi silversmithing by Margaret Nickelson Wright that identified the hallmarks used as signatures on the work. Choosing many which symbolized the weather, I enlarged and modified them to create the smaller designs. Baskets, jewelry, pottery, and woven rugs purchased for souvenirs inspired the larger designs.

PUEBLO RAIN
81" x 59", Shirley P. Kelly, Colden, NY, 2009.
Cottons, Quilters Dream Cotton batt, DMC Cotton machine embroidery thread, Sulky rayon thread, Superior King Tut 40 wt. Bottom Line thread; hand appliquéd, machine quilted.
2011.05.01

ANNETTE KENNEDY

As a military wife, Annette Kennedy has had the opportunity to live in several different states in the U.S. and in Puerto Rico. Amazed by the different landscapes, she loves nature and is inspired by its beauty. An amateur photographer, she combined that talent with her love of fabric and color, leading to her passion for creating landscape and pictorial quilts.

Annette's photograph of the Saint Catherine Chapel in Allenspark, Colorado inspired this quilt. "This chapel sits close to the road," she writes, "and is a well known landmark. It is a popular wedding site and is used for many holiday church services. It is a small church, but majestic and inspirational in sight."

AWARDS:
Moda
Best Wall Quilt
2009

MOUNTAIN CHAPEL
43" x 53", Annette Kennedy, Longmont, CO, 2008. Cottons; hand-painting with Setacolor on Prepared for Dyeing fabric; Sharpie marker; Quilter's Dream Cotton, select batting; cotton, silk, rayon, and polyester threads; raw-edge fused appliqué, painting, drawing, machine quilting.
2009.01.03

CHRIS KLEPPE

My quilts take their inspiration from old tile patterns and illuminated manuscripts.

I use interlace patterns to explore the intricacies of geometry.

In my work, hard-edged patterns contrast with the fluid qualities of nature.

MALTESE CROSS
76" x 88", Chris Kleppe, Milwaukee, WI, 1987. Cottons; hand and machine pieced and hand quilted.
1997.06.35

THERESA KLOSTERMAN

Filling time with beauty and practicality is the essence of Theresa's quilting efforts.

FLOWER BASKET SAMPLER
90" x 112", Theresa Klosterman, Mooreton, ND, 1984. Cottons and cotton blends; hand and machine pieced, hand quilted, and hand embroidered.
1997.06.23

AWARDS:
Third Place, Amateur Appliqué
1992

SUSAN KNIGHT

SATURN'S RINGS
61" x 41", Susan Knight, Bay Village, OH, 1986. Cottons and linen; hand pieced, hand appliquéd, and hand quilted. 1997.06.68

Susan enjoys sharing the utility and creativity of quiltmaking with others.

MARZENNA J. KROL

Having learned to quilt from Mennonites in the Lancaster, Pennsylvania, area, Marzenna gained her understanding of and appreciation for quiltmaking's artistry through their patience and love for the art.

BASKET OF FLOWERS
72" x 82", Marzenna J. Krol, Carmel Valley, CA, 1982. Cottons/polyesters; hand appliquéd and hand quilted.
1997.06.03

MARZENNA J. KROL

MAPLE LEAF
84" x 97", Marzenna J. Krol, Carmel Valley, CA, 1984. Cottons/ polyesters; hand appliquéd and hand quilted, machine pieced. 1997.06.37

TONI KRON

To ensure that each quilt she designs remains one-of-a-kind, Toni destroys the pattern once the project is complete to preserve its artistic integrity.

ORCHARD BEAUTY
88" x 105", Toni Kron, Guntersville, AL, 1986. Cottons, dacron/cotton blends; hand appliquéd, quilted, and embroidered.
1997.06.50

MARY E. KUEBLER

Quilting for Mary is not so much about achievement as it is a lifelong love of accomplishing beautiful, handmade items.

MANY STAR
77" x 96", Mary E. Kuebler, Cincinnati, OH, 1984. Cottons; batiked and hand quilted.
1997.06.36

Jan Lanahan

Quilting is but one entryway into the universe of textile artistry for Jan.

Baskets and the Corn
67" x 80", Jan Lanahan, Walkersville, MD, 1986. Cottons and linens; embroidered, hand painted, machine pieced, and hand quilted.
1992.07.01

AWARDS:
First Place
Theme: Baskets
1988

JAN LANAHAN

REACH FOR THE STARS
66" x 82", Jan Lanahan, Walkersville, MD, 1986. Cottons, flannels, satins; hand pieced and hand quilted.
1997.06.61

AWARDS:
Second Place
Innovative Pieced, Amateur
1987

JUDITH LARZELERE

I work abstractly and I am interested in setting up an ambiguous figure/ground dialogue through the manipulation of hue and value.

I feel committed to piecing because I see it as the most unique aspect of art making in this medium.

Form follows from the way that my quilts are made. Strip-piecing generates a non-pictorial, linear, abstract, non-geometric image by its process.

Piecing is what sets quilters apart from all other art media and allows us to generate images that no one else in their right mind would attempt.

To gain an individual artist's signature style is the goal of any professional; piecing gives those who rely on it a private aesthetic world to explore. For this reason I champion cutting and sewing.

RED SQUARED
59" x 59", Judith Larzelere, Westerly, RI, 1992. Cottons; machine pieced and quilted.
2008.01.01

JEAN RAY LAURY

LISTEN TO YOUR MOTHER
43" x 43", Jean Ray Laury, Clovis, CA, 1997. Cottons; hand screen printed and machine quilted.
2001.04.01

We all want to be remembered by our families, by descendents as yet unknown, and by our quilt communities. Our work is evidence of how we choose to be remembered.

The ties may be artistic or literary, profound or humorous, functional or aesthetic, but we want to leave something of ourselves.

My own work indicates a very personal perspective and expresses my need to see us laugh and to leave the world a more peaceful, exciting, and caring place in which to live.

LIBBY LEHMAN

When I make a quilt, it is first and foremost to please me. If I'm not happy with it, how can I expect anyone else to be? It is icing on the cake when others like my work, especially if they like it enough to buy it!

I would love for my quilts to be seen and admired for years to come. I try to use quality products and excellent workmanship. However, I won't be around to know what will happen years from today.

It gives me great pleasure to see my quilts hanging at The National Quilt Museum in the company of so many brilliant works of art. I know that ESCAPADE and STAR-CROSSED are in the hands of experts who will take great care of them. Thanks, guys

AWARDS:
First Place
Other Techniques
1993

ESCAPADE
80" x 80", Libby Lehman, Houston, TX, 1993. Cottons; rayon and metallic thread; machine pieced, machine embroidered, and machine quilted.
1997.07.09

LIBBY LEHMAN

STAR-CROSSED
70" x 70", Libby Lehman, Houston, TX, 1986. Cottons and cotton blends; machine pieced and hand quilted.
1997.06.76

SANDRA LEICHNER

I am passionate about the traditional American quilt, and that unique style is always reflected in my designs.

I fell in love with the original, elegant applique quilts of the Baltimore Album period and the infamous Emporia, Kansas, era. These quilts have had a profound impact on me and my approach to quilts and their design, as well as defining for me true artistry and craftsmanship when applied to the traditional art of quiltmaking.

My goal has always been to design and create one-of-a-kind hand appliqué quilts with careful attention to detail and workmanship. I like the test of translating the designs I see in my head into quilts that use challenging traditional quilt techniques to achieve a fresh updated look.

AWARDS:

RJR

Best Wall Quilt

2005

Collection of The National Quilt Museum

UNEXPECTED BEAUTY

51" x 67", Sandra Leichner, Albany, OR, 2004, Cottons; cotton, silk, and polyester threads; fabric paint, rock crystals, wool batting; hand and machine pieced; hand appliquéd, embroidered, and beaded; machine quilted.
2005.01.03

LILLIAN J. LEONARD

Competition is its own reward as Lillian creates quilts for contests.

TRANQUILITY
85" x 92", Lillian J. Leonard, Indianapolis, IN, 1985. Cottons; hand pieced, hand appliquéd, and hand quilted.
1997.06.85

LILLIAN J. LEONARD

TRANQUILITY (wallhanging)
34" x 34", Lillian J. Leonard, Indianapolis, IN, 1985.
1997.06.84

Marjorie Haight LYDECKER

SOMEWHERE IN TIME
90" x 90", Marjorie Haight Lydecker, Yarmouth Port, MA, 2001. Cottons; machine pieced, hand appliquéd, hand embroidered, hand quilted.
2012.01.01

A pattern purchased in 1983 was the inspiration for the design of this quilt in 1993. Marjorie Haight Lydecker became enthusiastic about Jacobean designs when a student transposed crewel bedhanging designs into appliqué patterns.

"Although the shape of the tree, flowers, and leaves follows the original, nothing else is the same," writes Marjorie. "Broderie perse in leaves, birds, flowers, tree trunk, butterflies, and a rooster are my additions. Instead of ordinary hummocks I designed a base for the tree and, using 40 fabrics, formed a base for the center. The quilt was then put aside for four years.

"Some of the borders were adapted from a Jacobean bed hanging that was done in crewel work. The large flowers were hand quilted and embroidered before being appliquéd to the quilt."

Sharon Malec

Barking Up the Wrong Tree

58" x 45", Sharon Malec, West Chicago, IL, 1999. Cottons and cotton blends; hand painted, machine appliquéd, machine couched, and machine quilted. 2000.04.01

As a quilt artist, I have a love of fabrics. It is a wonderfully colorful and tactile medium, resulting in art work with a soft expression. I am particularly drawn to nature's colors which complement the animal and nature themes that dominate my work. A variety of hand and machine techniques are used to create my quilts.

AWARDS:
Third Place
Theme Wall: Dogwoods
2000

Marguerite Ann

MALWITZ

DESERT DUSK

53" x 43", Marguerite Ann Malwitz, Brookfield, CT, 1988. Cottons, blends, silks, and satins; cotton and metallic threads; tie-dyed, machine and hand pieced, hand quilted.
1997.07.06

Sharing her life's journey as a Christian artist is the focus of Marguerite's studio art quiltmaking.

Inge MARDAL & Steen HOUGS

IT'S NOT SUMMER YET
54" x 41", Inge Mardal, Brussels, Belgium, 2000. Cottons; hand appliquéd, machine embroidered, and machine quilted.
2001.13.01

The way we work makes each quilt a part of a continuum, building on previous experience and guided by new ideas for realization of the next piece.

We process intellectually and artistically what we see of interest and are open for new inspiration. We consequently do not have preconceived ideas on which directions to follow in terms of motifs, styles, or techniques.

It will be very exciting to see to where that will be leading us.

AWARDS:
RJR
Best Wall Quilt
2001

Inge MARDAL & Steen HOUGS

SUN-BATHING BLUE TIT
66" x 80", Inge Mardal, Chantilly, France, 2003. Cottons; hand painted and machine quilted.
2004.01.03

AWARDS:
RJR
Best Wall Quilt
2004

SUZANNE MARSHALL

An image from the past, thumbing through a library book, or walking down the street of a foreign city may plant a seed in my mind that may inspire a quilt.

Starting with this small inspiration, a quilt may begin without my knowing how it will evolve.

As I work, the quilt itself helps me know what to do next.

The finished quilt is always a surprise, often surpassing any initial concept.

AWARDS:
Timeless Treasures
Hand Workmanship
2002

MOTHER'S DAY
81" x 81", Suzanne Marshall, Clayton, MO, 2001. Cottons; hand appliquéd, hand embroidered, and hand quilted.
2002.01.01

SUZANNE MARSHALL

TOUJOURS NOUVEAU
69" x 80", Suzanne Marshall, Clayton, MO, 1993. Cottons; hand appliquéd with embroidery and hand quilted. Named one of the 100 Best American Quilts of the 20th Century.
1996.01.27

AWARDS:
Gingher
Hand Workmanship
1993

JUDY MARTIN

"SUMMER LAKE LOG CABIN combines two traditional Log Cabin blocks in different sizes and colorings," writes Judy Martin. "The innovation comes from the combination of traditional elements. The six-inch blocks are colored to make spirals. The nine-inch blocks are divided along the diagonal into dark and light halves. I used four small blocks in the quilt center, adding logs around them so they would fit the large blocks. The rest of the quilt center comprises the larger blocks. The small blocks form an inner pieced border. A log border completes the composition."

Over the years, Judy has made numerous Log Cabins that are, like this quilt, slight variations of the traditional pattern. She began quilting in 1969, and worked for *Quilter's Newsletter Magazine* from 1979 to 1987. SUMMER LAKE LOG CABIN is from Judy's book *Judy Martin's Log Cabin Quilt Book.*

SUMMER LAKE LOG CABIN
72" x 90", designed and machine pieced by Judy Martin, Grinnell, IA, 2007. Machine quilted by Margy Sieck. Cottons.
2013.05.01

Katie Pasquini Masopust

I hope to create beautiful, thought-provoking art quilts for the viewers, but mainly I make them because that is how I express my creative energies.

I love working on every aspect of the quiltmaking process.

Making art quilts makes me happy.

Teneramente (with Tender Emotion)
50" x 63", Katie Pasquini Masopust, Santa Fe, NM, 2006. Cottons, satin, Ultrasuede; transparent, cotton, and polyester threads; wool batting. Machine appliquéd and quilted. 2007.03.01

Collection of The National Quilt Museum

NORIKO MASUI

Intricacy of design and workmanship excellence guide Noriko's artistry, which is inspired by daily life as well as spiritual interests.

AWARDS:
First Place
Mixed Techniques
1997

A MANDALA OF FLOWERS
76" x 81", Noriko Masui, Saitama, Japan, 1997. Cottons, silks, polyesters, and materials from Japanese kimonos and obis; hand pieced, hand appliquéd, and hand quilted.
1998.04.01

JEAN K. MATHEWS

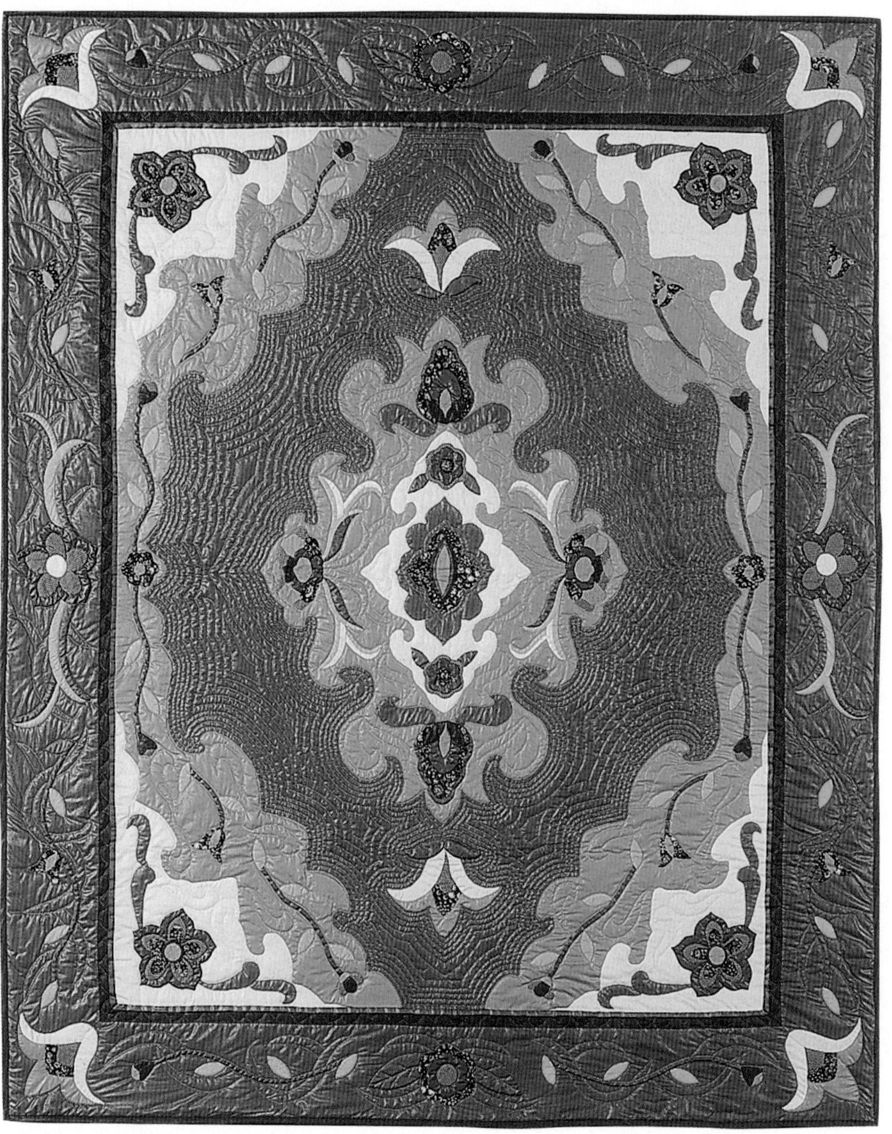

PERSIAN PARADISE

59" x 72½", Jean K. Mathews, Marco Island, FL, 1986. Cottons and polyester/cotton chintz; hand appliquéd, reverse appliquéd, and hand quilted.
1997.06.55

In thinking about what I hope to achieve in quiltmaking, I must reflect on the 28 years since I began making quilts.

It is amazing to think back to cutting with templates only, hand piecing and quilting, and uninspiring fabrics. Today we have wonderful rotary cutters, ¼" presser feet, the artistry of free-motion quilting, and best of all, the beautiful fabrics, great magazines, shops, and fantastic shows to inspire us.

Being fulfilled with pushing my creativity to new limits, the satisfaction of having my work in shows, and helping others to learn, along with the gratitude and praise my family bestows on me every time I make a quilt for them, has been wonderful. I hope I am given good health to achieve more of the same.

LAVERNE N. MATHEWS

Total immersion in every aspect of quilting, from collecting to production to appreciation of others' work, informs Laverne's approach to quiltmaking.

STRAWBERRY SUNDAE
64" x 83", Laverne N. Mathews, Orange, TX, 1986. Cottons and cotton blends; hand appliquéd and hand quilted.
1997.06.78

AWARDS:
Second Place
Appliqué, Amateur
1987

LAVERNE N. MATHEWS

TAOS TAPESTRY

37" x 40", Laverne N. Mathews, Orange, TX, 1986. Cottons and cotton blends; machine pieced and hand quilted.
1997.06.81

JUDY MATHIESON

Quilt making has been very rewarding for me, creatively and professionally.

I enjoy the process and the result. I hope that others enjoy my quilts, but I make them for myself.

Being able to teach quilt making has allowed me to travel far beyond my expectations and to meet wonderful people.

NEW DIRECTIONS
76" x 92", Judy Mathieson, Sebastopol, CA, 1996. Cottons; machine pieced, and hand and machine quilted. 2001.07.01

KARIN MATTHIESEN

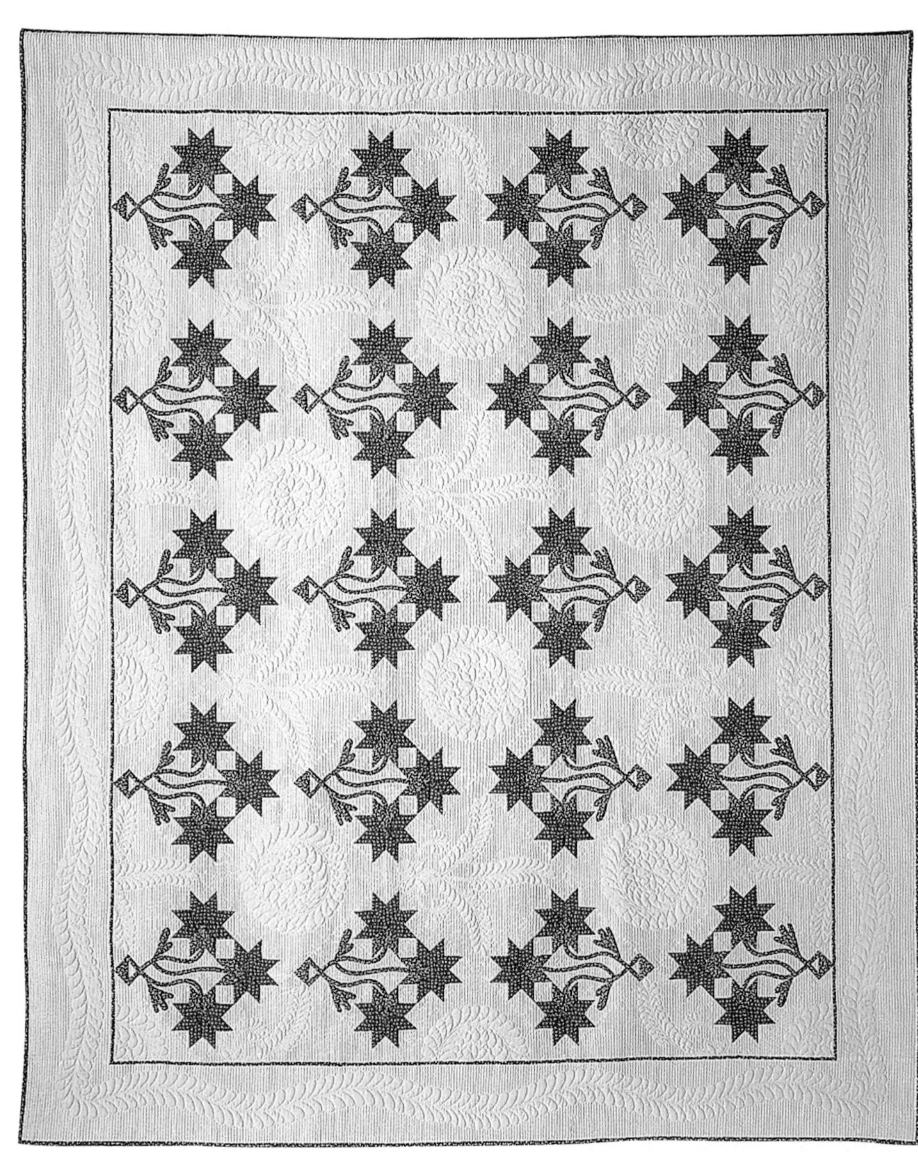

Appliqué was her initial inspiration to start quilting; a desire to achieve excellent workmanship and try new styles and techniques guides Karin's current efforts.

BED OF PEONIES
85" x 96", Karin Matthiesen, Madison, WI, 1986. Cottons; hand appliquéd and hand quilted.
1996.01.04

AWARDS:

Gingher
Hand Workmanship
1986

First Place
Traditional Patchwork,
Professional
1986

THERESE MAY

"I like the idea of Life being the flow of the creative process," writes Therese May. "Every thought I think and every activity I engage in is creative and has some result."

On the top section of LIFE ON THREE LEVELS, Therese has placed her "Flying Saucers" to represent the Universal level of life. "The middle level is the physical, suggesting the transformational nature of our life on the planet. The two profiles on the bottom of the quilt represent the dreamers. In the center is a cone-shaped container with a pink streamer which carries the dreams and ideas back to the top, giving us a continuation of the creative process."

LIFE ON THREE LEVELS
66" x 67", Therese May, San Jose, CA, 1995. Fabric, thread, acrylic paint, fabric paint, buttons, beads, painted panels, braids, polymer clay; machine appliqué, hand embellished, hand quilted.
2011.01.01

MARY JO MCCABE

Achievement is a combination of effort, learning new skills, and artistry.

STARRY, STARRY NIGHT
75" x 90", Mary Jo McCabe, Davenport, IA, 1985. Cottons; hand pieced and hand quilted.
1997.06.77

SUE MCCARTY

"Inspired by J. R. R. Tolkien's *The Hobbit*, this wholecloth quilt is my attempt to depict some of the events that await the unsuspecting hobbit, Bilbo Baggins," writes Sue McCarty. "Some of you may ask, 'Where are the dwarves?' Due to limited space, I have chosen to represent them in three subtle ways. First, there are 13 musical instruments tangled among the floral vine which serves as a border between the blocks. Second, there are 13 barrels on the lake-town dock, each the color of a dwarf cloak. Third, there are 15 crystals on the eagle's saddle, 13 of which are for the dwarves with one each for Gandolf and Bilbo.

"This quilt is meant to foretell just some of the adventures awaiting Bilbo and thus spark an interest in *The Hobbit*. For those who are true fans of the great writer's work, please enjoy this quilted offering and forgive any artistic license forced by the limitations of space and stitching."

AWARDS:
APQS Longarm Machine Quilting Award
2013

ADVENTURE AWAITS
88" x 80", Sue McCarty, Roy, UT, 2012. Cottons, Swarovski crystals. Longarm machine quilted.
2013.06.05

SUE MCCARTY

HARMONY WITHIN

71" x 81", Sue McCarty, Roy, UT, 2011. Cottons, black 60/40 cotton/poly Winline batting, 100% bamboo Winline batting, 4,200 Swarovski crystals, Paintstiks, Czechoslovakian vintage beaded trim. Threads: Yenmet Metallic; Monrex Metallic; Superior Metallic King Tut, Bottom Line, So-Fine, Kimono Silk, and Razzle Dazzle; YLI variegated. Longarm machine quilted. 2012.02.01

A Japanese Garden inspired the story of two different beings who find harmony within the bonds of marriage.

The dragon represents the more right-brained creature. She prefers to live her life in the world of art and literature, foregoing more practical matters. Yet, despite her preference to live among the clouds, she firmly holds the key to a heart which belongs to the fisherman. With his left-brained approach to life, he maintains a detailed account of practical matters on his abacus and is steadfast in his need to build a steady, secure future.

The center of the quilt represents their union. The largest pagoda is the home they share, while the two smaller structures represent the individual space they both need. Two fenghuang (Chinese birds of good omen) overlook the scene, bringing peace and prosperity to both fisherman and dragon.

AWARDS:

Janome Best of Show

2012

Collection of The National Quilt Museum

SUE McCARTY

The inspiration for this quilt came soon after my brother, a long time admirer of J. R. R. Tolkien, convinced me to read the literary masterpiece *The Lord of the Rings*.

The centerpiece of the quilt to depict Aragorn's ultimate victory over the enemy, his coronation as the king of Gondor and his marriage to Arwen. Also present is my representation of the white wizard Gandalf. The horses of Rohan, along with the tree and horn of Gondor, stand for the world of men. The Gate of Moria is for the dwarves. You can find many other characters depicted in the quilt too.

The One Ring dominates the upper feathered border. Within the ring are the elfish words which translate "One Ring to rule them all."

AWARDS:
Janome Best of Show
2010

Tribute to Tolkien
85" x 90", Sue McCarty, Roy, UT, 2010. Cottons, Swarovski crystals; longarm machine quilted. National Quilting Association Masterpiece Quilt.
2010.03.01

MARSHA MCCLOSKEY

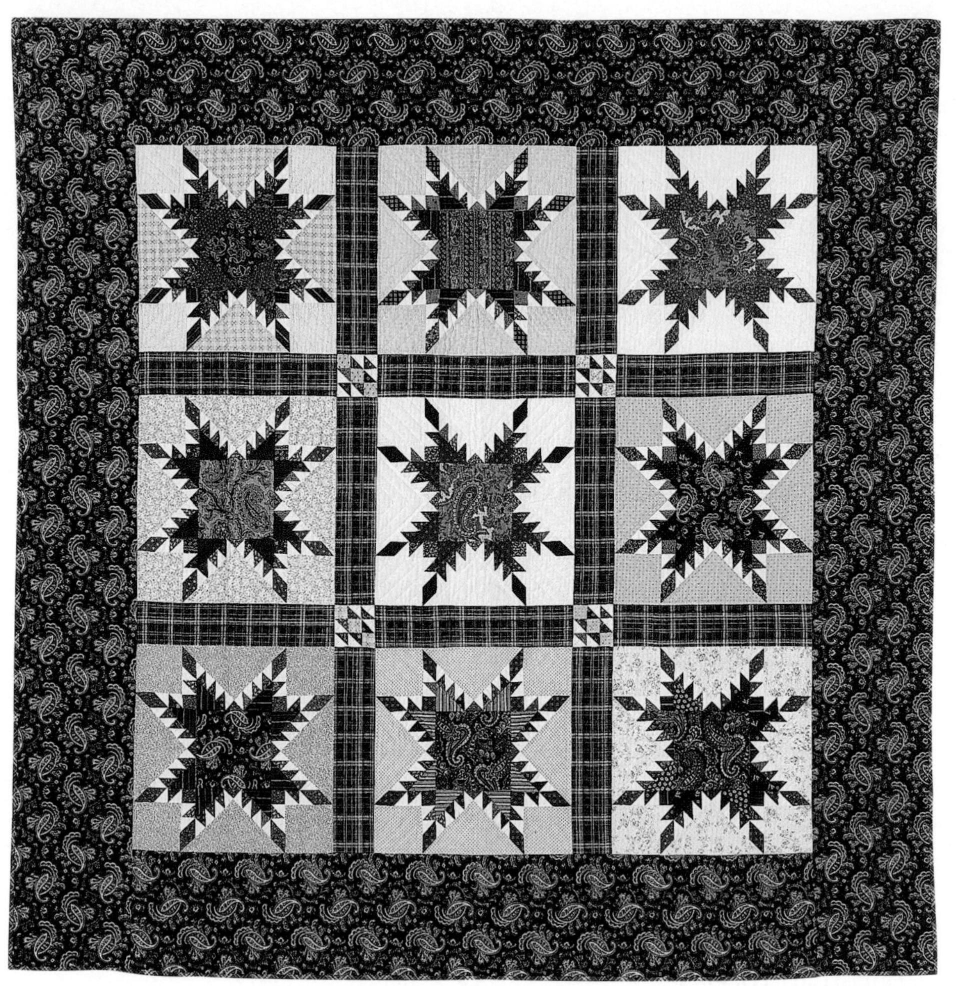

True artistry in one's craft is achievement at the highest level.

STAR OF CHAMBLIE
67" x 67", Marsha McCloskey, Seattle, WA, 1986. Cottons; machine pieced and hand quilted.
2001.05.01

Ruth B. McDowell

Like an artist in any medium, I make my artwork because it is personally exhilarating to do.

My quilts express who I am and what interests me. They communicate that excitement and personal expression to many other people.

The process of working in this medium is endlessly fascinating. It's a journey with many passages, interweavings, forks in the road, and an unknown ending.

The tactile quality of fibers, the endlessly varied patterns and glorious subtleties of color, the physical movements involved in cutting and sewing—all are unique to the medium. The association of the fabrics to other lives and places is a source of contemplation.

Creation, exhilaration, self-expression, communication, tactile pleasure, visual treats, meditation, and contemplation are achievements that very few careers produce.

Na Pali

70" x 77", Ruth B. McDowell, Winchester, MA,1999. Cottons; machine pieced, hand-appliquéd boat, and machine quilted.
2001.06.01

DORRIS MCMANIS

OMAN
11½" x 14", Dorris McManis, St. Louis, MO, 2007. Cottons, fusible web, fabric pen; machine appliqué, fused appliqué, machine embroidery, hand quilted, fabric drawing. Seventy-seven footies were donated by Dorris' husband Charles (Chuck) McManis. One was donated by his mother, Ruth Rowland McManis.
F2012.03.47

In 2007, Dorris McManis challenged herself to create a 12" x 12" quilt each week for a year. She did this "just for myself, to be creative and to do something I would not normally do with fabric." She wrote that these small quilts "reflect the influences of places I have visited, books I have read, and quilters that inspired me." In October 2007, Dorris took a 14 month "sabbatical" from her footie project, which she resumed during the first week of January, 2009.

"In every artist's life there is a moment of quickening where a medium, a teacher, a technique or a burning question takes hold." This happened to Dorris when she saw the Quilt National innovative quilt exhibit in 1991 in St. Louis. "Quilting became a lifelong passion, course of meticulous study and outlet for an ever-deepening creative force."

Dorris passed away in 2010.

KEIKO MINAMI

Using her graphic design background, Keiko took over two years to create this stunning hand-pieced-and-quilted entry with a combination of diamond and hexagon shapes. Multiple fabrics of varying values of pinks and lavenders create the lush rose blossoms and buds with extensive use of shadow trapunto in the alternating blocks. The combination of several shades of off-white adds subtle complexity to the background. Although the hexagons appear more prominent, Keiko hopes viewers note the diamonds as well seeing as this quilt began with a little diamond and "just kept growing."

Keiko says since her mother taught her "you can tell a real quilter by the back of her work," she paid special attention to the reverse side of her quilt to ensure it would hang straight and true.

AWARDS:
AQS
Hand Workmanship Award
2013

THE CHARM OF SMALL PINK ROSES
79" x 86", Keiko Minami, Kawanishi, Hyogo, Japan, 2012. Cottons; hand pieced, hand appliquéd, hand quilted, hand trapunto.
2013.06.02

KEIKO MIYAUCHI

BLUE EARTH FILLED WITH WATER AND FLOWERS
76" x 83", Keiko Miyauchi, Nagano, Japan, 2000. Hand-dyed cottons, polyester; hand appliquéd, trapuntoed, and hand quilted.
2001.12.01

I have loved floral quilts ever since seeing the Whitehill Collection quilts at the Denver Museum in 1986. I've made floral quilts ever since.

Roses, cosmos, Gerbera daisies, and lilies, along with animals, populate my quilts. I try to sew with passion and precision.

I hope my quilts speak to the need to care for our planet's flowers and animals.

Hopefully my quilts make people happy, stay in their minds, and encourage them to become quiltmakers, too.

AWARDS:
Timeless Treasures
Hand Workmanship
2001

Keiko Miyauchi

"I began making quilts in 1981," writes Keiko Miyauchi. "I have been making quilts and teaching quilting ever since. I entered a quilt in the American Quilter's Society contest for the first time in 1993. Since then, whenever I make a quilt, I enter it. I already have seven dogwood ribbons [first place awards]. Recently some of my pupils have won awards in Japan and the United States. I'm proud of them."

When Keiko designed this quilt, she wanted to add something to the roses. At the time she saw a picture of French buildings with iron lace at the windows. This inspired her to create her blue fence. It is a lovely way to surround her favorite flowers in her favorite colors.

A Rose Garden in a Blue Fence
81" x 81", Keiko Miyauchi, Nagano, Japan, 2008. Cottons, polyester batting, polyester thread; and appliquéd, trapunto, hand quilted.
2009.01.02

AWARDS:

American Quilter's Society
Hand Workmanship
2009

Barbara Pettinga
MOORE

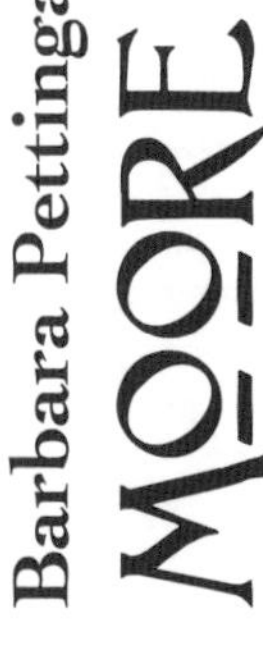

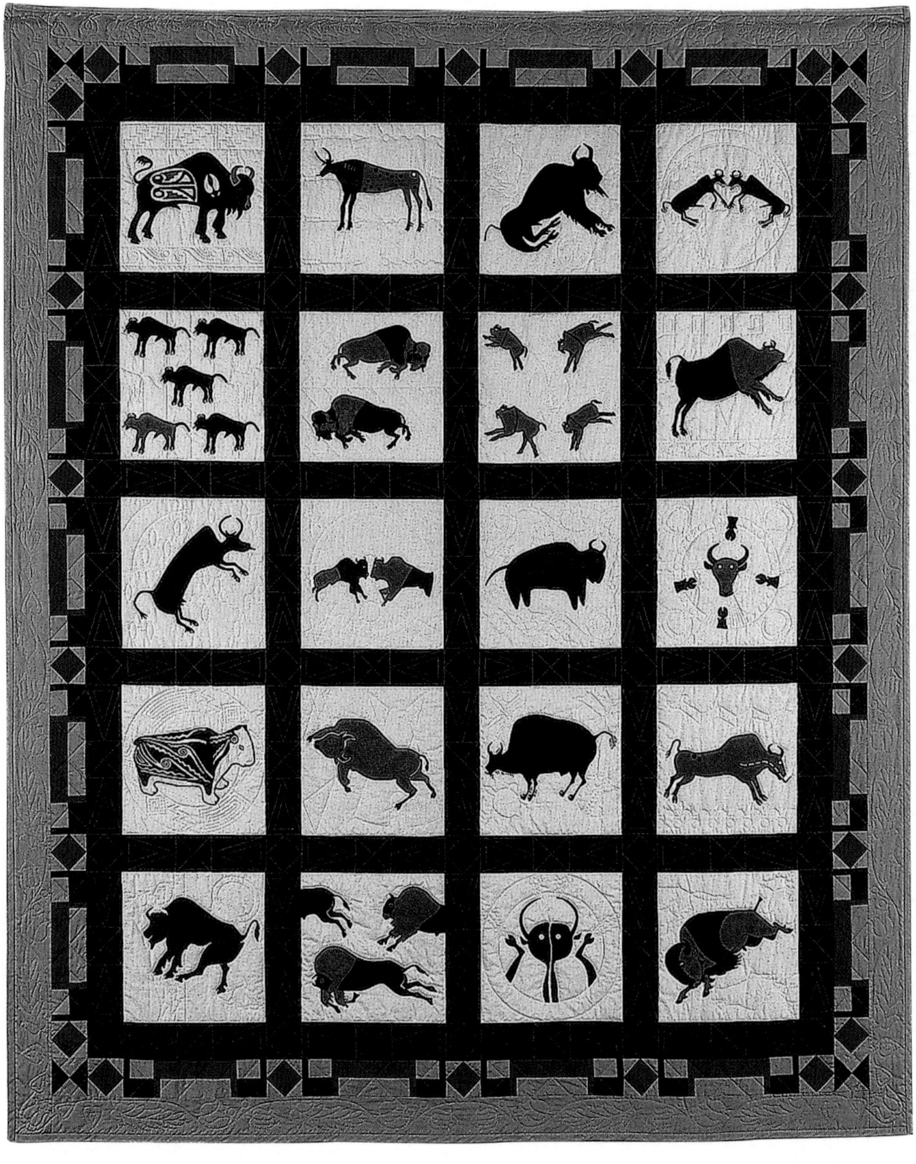

Combining a love for and background in art and science, especially wildlife, lies at the heart of Barbara's approach to quiltmaking and other artistic endeavors.

BUFFALO MAGIC
75" x 90", Barbara Pettinga Moore, Shelburne, VT, 1984. Cotton/poly blend, suede cloth; hand appliquéd and hand quilted.
1997.06.09

AWARDS:
First Quilt
1986

CARON L. MOSEY

Carole Adams
Mona Barker
Linda Cantrell
Rhoda Cohen
Shannie J. Coyne
Pat Cox
Barbara Crane
Joe Cunningham
Ronnie Durrance
Elly Dyson
Chris Wolf Edmonds
Victoria Faoro
Lee Farrington
Cathy Grafton
Roberta Horton
Lois K. Ide
Jean Johnson
Ed Larson (with Sarah Hass)
Masami Kato
Helen Kelly
Donna Makim
Gwen Marston
Judy Mathieson
Carolyn Muller
Paula Nadelstern
Dawn Rappold
Art Salemme
Steve Schutt
Joan Schulze
Elaine Sparlin
Susan Turbak
Emma Martin Yost

Artists from The Progressive Pictorial Quilt
Caron L. Mosey, coordinator

The Progressive Pictorial Quilt
44" x 44", artists in *America's Pictorial Quilts*, coordinated by Caron L. Mosey, 1987. Cottons and cotton blends; hand appliquéd, embroidered, and quilted; machine pieced.
1991.01.01

CYNTHIA MORGAN

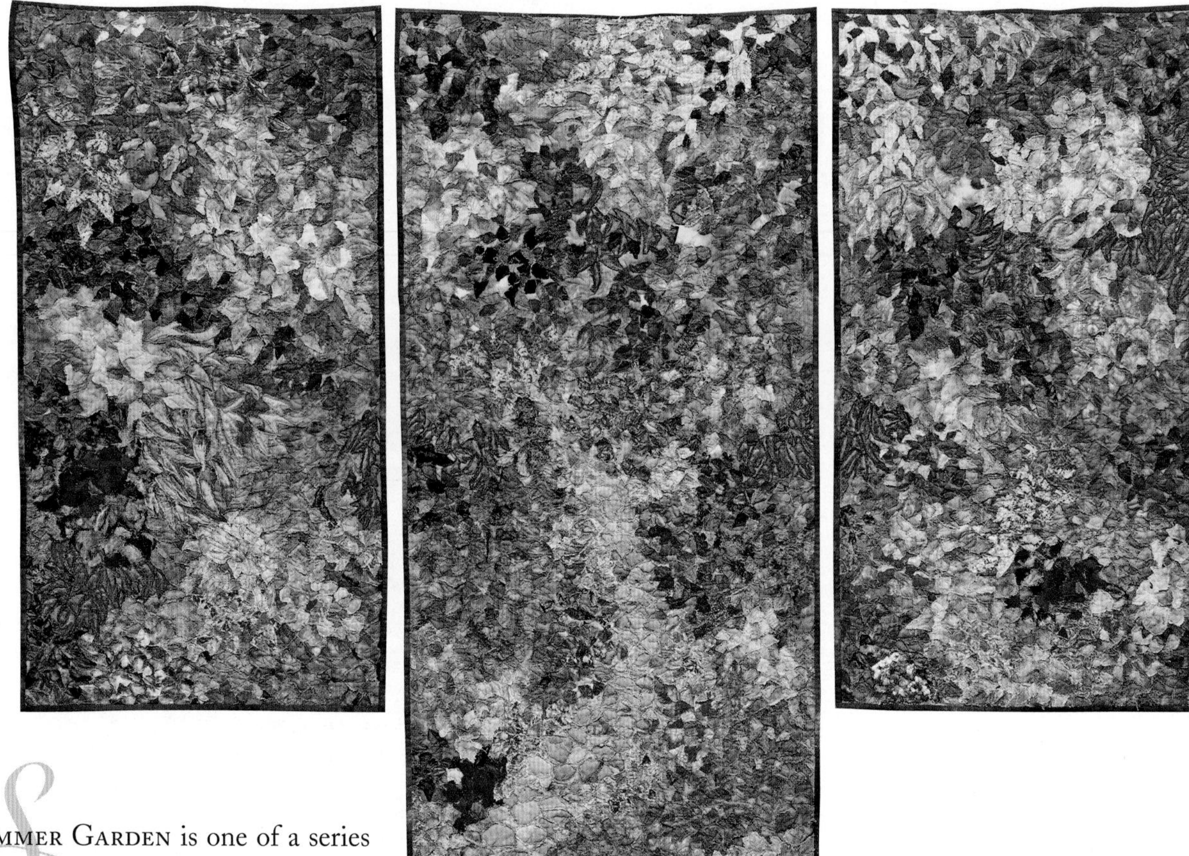

SUMMER GARDEN is one of a series of garden impressions. It was designed intuitively, working with small remnants of dyed fabrics to create the impression of a walkway through a beautiful garden.

Cynthia uses photographs taken during holidays with her husband in the Australian rainforest, outback or barrier reef as the jumping off point for her designs. Through her quilts she wants to make the viewer more aware of the beauty of the natural environment that is being gradually eroded by man's uncontrolled intrusion.

SUMMER GARDEN (TRIPTYCH)
59" x 46", Cynthia Morgan, Queensland, Australia, 2003. Hand-dyed cotton, silk and polyester organza; layered, machine quilted.
2011.08.01

Mary Morgan

Being a self-taught quilter has given Mary deep respect for quilters who made beautiful quilts without formal art training or unlimited, inspirational supplies. She is more concerned with what her quilts do than what they say.

Diffractions III
65" x 94", Mary Morgan, Little Rock, AR, 1989. Hand-dyed cottons; machine pieced and hand quilted.
1997.06.16

LAURA MURRAY

HELIACAL RISE
71" x 74", Laura Murray, Minneapolis, MN, 1996. Cottons and silks; hand painted, hand and machine pieced, and machine quilted.
1997.03.01

My artistic aspirations can be described as similar to the *Star Trek* mission: "Boldly going where no one has gone before."

It is the process of experimentation and the joy of discovery that excites me.

The work of my hands is essential to my well-being, with the objective always to make something that is unique and beautiful.

I use my curiosity and creativity to seek new possibilities in my ongoing adventures with textile art.

AWARDS:
RJR
Best Wall Quilt
1997

JOYCE MURRIN

BEACH ROSES
79" x 49", Joyce Murrin, Orient, NY, 1986.
Cottons and cotton blends, some hand dyed; machine pieced and hand quilted.
1997.06.05

My greatest joy in quiltmaking is the challenge—met head on and accomplished.

Whether it's refusing to compensate a line in the design or fighting my self to keep a color or particular fabric in the process and maybe losing in the end, it's all worth the challenge!

My desire to design pieced quilts with many non-traditional angles has been my most rewarding challenge. I met that technical challenge by working until I perfected setting in any angle, using any fabric, easily.

Now I have the freedom to be creative, to think and design artistically, and in the end, to make quilts from my own designs that are complex yet visually uncomplicated; still challenging; sometimes surprising; and for many reasons, pleasing to me.

CLAUDIA CLARK MYERS

WHO'S YOUR POPPY?
61" x 62", Claudia Clark Myers, Duluth, MN, 2001. Cottons; machine paper pieced, machine appliquéd, machine embroidered, and machine quilted.
2002.02.01

The quilts that I make are always the culmination of much agonizing and mind-changing.

There never seems to be a straight path from first idea to last stitch.

I want my quilts to be objects of curiosity to the viewer, not just one-glance wonders. My hope is that the viewer will be intrigued and spend some time looking at my quilts, puzzling over how I did that, or WHY I did that.

I also would like to inspire viewers to try something different—to carry away some small seed that will blossom into a new direction for their own work. That's what I hope to achieve!

AWARDS:
RJR
Best Wall Quilt
2002

JAN MYERS-NEWBURY

Known for her work with geometrics and shibori dyeing techniques, Jan's art is also informed by pattern.

PRECIPICE
75" x 93", Jan Myers-Newbury, Pittsburgh, PA, 1989. Hand dyed cottons; machine pieced and machine quilted.
2001.08.01

Philippa Naylor

Flower Power
62" x 65", Philippa Naylor, Beverley, East Yorkshire, UK, 2008. Cottons, cotton batting; machine embroidered, machine quilted.
2009.01.05

Philippa Naylor has two other quilts in The National Quilt Museum collection; both are pieced quilts. She decided to try a whole cloth quilt thinking it might not be quite so complicated and demanding. Flower Power is the result. "It was more difficult, I think, to do a whole cloth quilt," says Philippa. "You have to create all the interest with just the quilting, and that isn't as simple as it sounds."

Flower Power is a subtle quilt, with delicate shades of yellow, green, and orange. These shades are created solely by the quilting thread and the sun and floral machine embroidery Philippa stitched on the white top fabric before layering the quilt together and quilting it.

AWARDS:
Bernina
Machine Workmanship
2009

PHILIPPA NAYLOR

I make quilts because I love to sew and quilting satisfies my creative needs!

I want to draw the viewer in with a large dramatic design. Then I want them to come close, study the detail, and understand how much pleasure I get from making a quilt, maybe inspire them to have a go at stitching any way they want.

If the viewer is never going to sew, I'd like them to go away from my quilt feeling that their day is brighter and better because of what they have just seen.

My aims are to continue to explore and develop my work, to improve, to keep enjoying it all (even the boring repetitive bits!), and to continue to share what I do with others.

AWARDS:
Hancock's of Paducah
Best of Show
2003

LIME LIGHT
81" x 81," Philippa Naylor, Dhahran, Saudi Arabia, 2002. Hand-dyed and painted cottons; machine pieced, trapuntoed, and machine quilted.
2003.01.01

PHILIPPA NAYLOR

POP STARS
86" x 86," Philippa Naylor, Dhahran, Saudi Arabia, 2002. Hand-dyed cottons; machine pieced, trapuntoed, and machine quilted.
2002.03.01

AWARDS:
Bernina
Machine Workmanship
2002

JULIA OVERTON NEEDHAM

Before she passed away, Julia reflected that quiltmaking was only a hobby for her. The only quilt she did not keep is the one in the collection.

TENNESSEE PINK MARBLE
72" x 88", Julia Overton Needham, Knoxville, TN, 1990. Cottons, cotton blends; hand pieced, appliquéd, and quilted.
1996.01.26

AWARDS:
Gingher
Hand Workmanship
1991

Barbara Newman

Stardust
88" x 88", Barbara Newman, Brandon, MS, 2007. Cottons; hand pieced, appliquéd, and quilted.
2008.04.01

My love for the art of quiltmaking began in 1991. As I made my first quilt, I knew I had found my creative inspiration.

From that day forward my hope was to create handmade quilts that would continue the tradition of our mothers and grandmothers. I strive to achieve the ability to make quilts of my own design and my version of antique quilts that have inspired me.

What I hope to achieve through the artistry of quiltmaking is to inspire those quilters who view my work to experience the joy of creating quilts by hand, and to leave a legacy to my children and grandchildren that they can hold and know that my love for them was stitched into each quilt.

Awards:
AQS
Hand Workmanship
2008

HALLIE O'KELLEY

Hallie's artistry is a combination of using hand-dyed fabric, silk screening some fabrics, judicious use of photographs, and intricate hand-stitched quilting.

ZINNIAS IN THE WINDOWS OF MY LOG CABIN
77" x 85", Hallie H. O'Kelley, Tuscaloosa, AL, 1987. Cottons; machine pieced and hand quilted.
1997.06.34

AWARDS:
Second Place
Theme: Log Cabin
1987

ANNE J. OLIVER

MOMMA'S GARDEN
88" x 91", Anne J. Oliver, Alexandria, VA, 1992. Cottons; hand appliquéd and hand quilted.
1996.01.19

It was my fervent desire to reach the frustrated quilter who just might find ways to get over quilting hurdles by using freezer paper in the creation of quality quilts. All of my work has been done with the aid of freezer paper. More often than not, freezer paper took me over rough spots without losing that quality.

I firmly believe I would not have created award-winning quilts if I had not taken freezer paper out of the kitchen and put it into the sewing room. It helped me to compete with the "Big Boys." It made me more creative, gave me lots of fun, eliminated my frustrations, and brought me new friends from many places. FREEZER PAPER, take a bow, you did good!

AWARDS:
AQS
Best of Show
1992

ANNE J. OLIVER

"PAINTED METAL CEILING is my version of a cheap tin ceiling, around 1905," says Anne Oliver. "It was found in homes, especially dining and living rooms, also bars and five-and-tens. Usually tin ceilings covered bad ceilings or walls, or both. My husband, Bob, gave me the idea of using subdued colors. He did demolition work while in college and saw colored tin ceilings. The tin plates were usually about 24 inch x 24 inch.

"Design is everywhere in my work. The designs are simple, with ornate hand quilting to create depth in the work. Tin ceilings were strongly American architecture."

PAINTED METAL CEILING
80" x 80", Anne J. Oliver, Tacoma, WA, 1988. Cottons; machine pieced, hand appliquéd, and hand quilted
2009.02.01

AWARDS:

Named one of the 100 Best Quilts of the 20th Century

ANNE J. OLIVER

Roses in the Round
80" x 80", Anne J. Oliver, Tacoma, WA, 1993. Commercial cottons; hand appliquéd, and hand quilted.
2009.02.02

This magnificent memorial quilt to her husband is the last quilt Bob and Anne Oliver worked on together. Bob's impeccable attention to detail and composition and Anne's incredible skill in needlecrafts has produced a fitting memorial quilt to their union.

Look closely at Roses in the Round and you will see the incredible quilting for which Anne is so well known. Anne divides her quilts into quarters and quilts one quarter at a time.

NANCY OTA

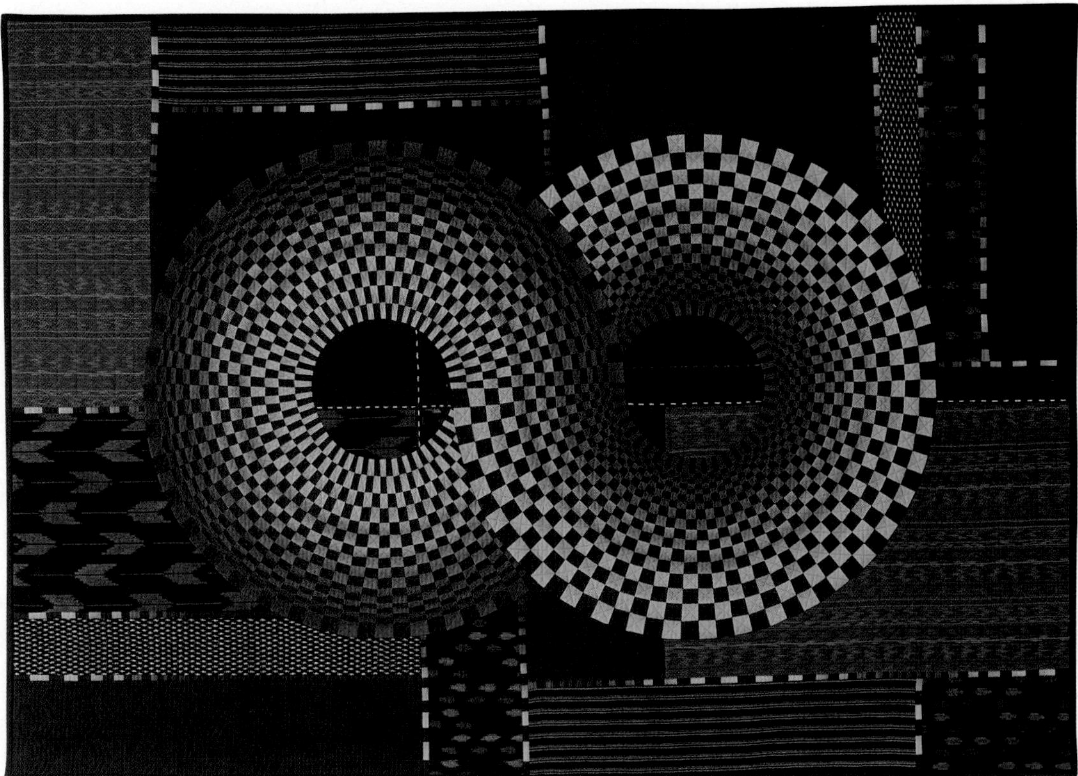

The entire process of creating a quilt is "sew" much fun:

• shopping—feeling and seeing the tempting colors and prints;

• viewing photos and paintings and imagining how they might translate into a quilt;

• traveling and composing photos to inspire future designs; and

• playing with color and textures while dyeing fabric.

Creating quilts allows me to use my favorite objects—needle, fabric, color, and thread—my senses, and my imagination.

I hope to touch the viewer with my vision: What does the viewer see from a distance and up close? How might the viewer use what I have done to create something new and original?

INFINITY
58" x 40", Nancy Ota, San Clemente, CA, 2005. Cottons, cotton/linen, yukata (cotton kimono) fabric; machine pieced, hand appliquéd, sashiko, machine quilted.
2006.06.01

AWARDS:
Moda
Best Wall Quilt
2006

BETTY K. PATTY

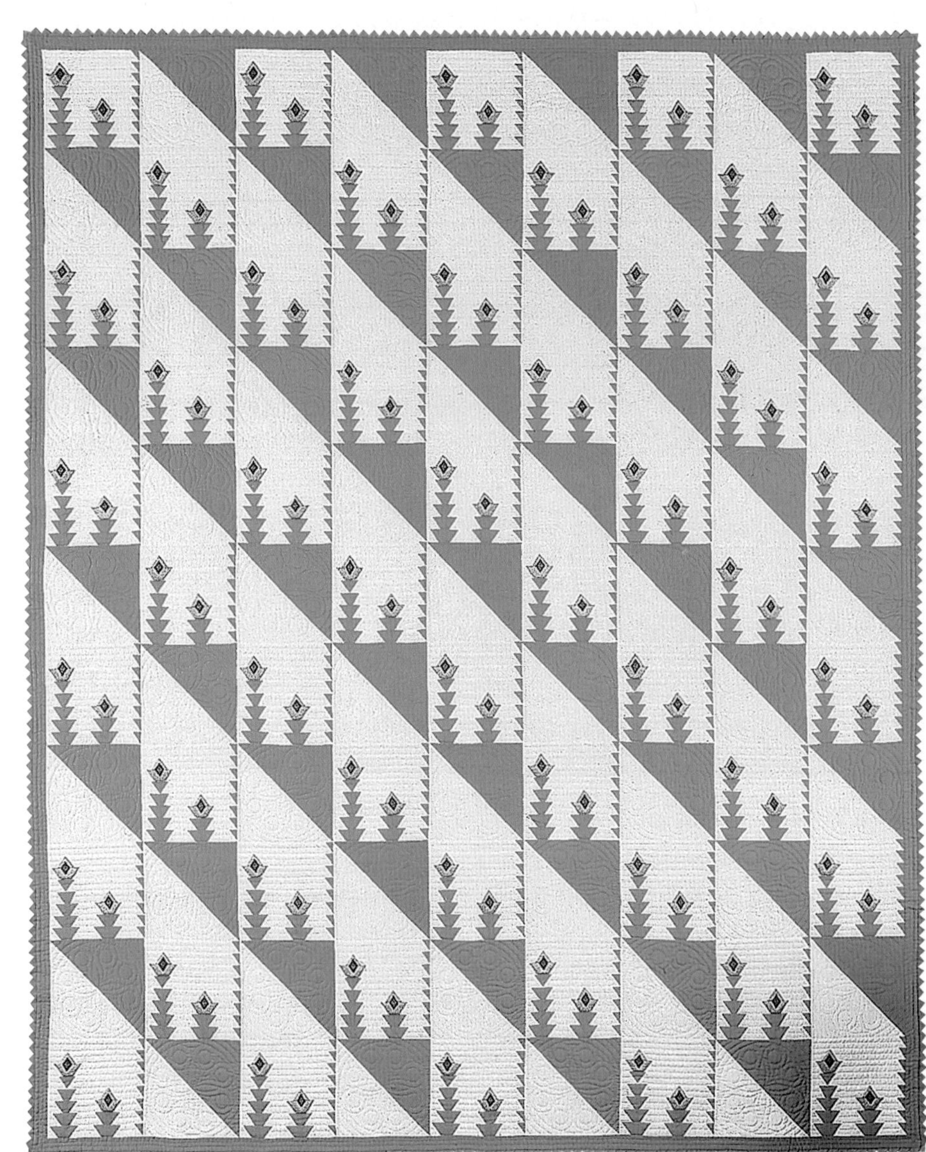

My interest in quilting has not lessened, although I lost my best friend and supporter, husband Dale, in 2003. It was good to have my quilting to fall back on.

I have slowed down creating full-sized hand quilted pieces and am making/donating crib quilts with three other members of our "Four Squares" group. The quilts are given to the Dayton (Ohio) Children's Hospital We have well surpassed the 1,000th quilt now and are still counting.

I did win some honors from the Ohio Bicentennial contest in 2003 with a quilt that is now in the Ohio Historical Museum.

I still tell my friends to enter the AQS Show at Paducah, as it is such an exciting contest to be involved with.

COUNTRY GARDEN
80" x 96", Betty K. Patty, Bradford, OH, 1985. Cottons; machine pieced, hand appliquéd, and hand quilted with trapunto.
1997.06.14

JOYCE B. PEADEN

A love of history, including quilt history and placing current events into historical context, and devotion to family are the focus of Joyce's quiltmaking.

MOUNT ST. HELENS, DID YOU TREMBLE?
79" x 95", Joyce B. Peaden, Prosser, WA, 1991. Cottons, metallic fabrics; hand and machine appliquéd, machine pieced, Seminole pieced, and hand quilted.
1991.02.01

SYLVIA PICKELL

ESCAPE FROM CIRCLE CITY
76" x 86", Sylvia Pickell, Sumter, SC, 1986. Cottons and poly blends; machine pieced, hand appliquéd, and hand quilted.
1997.06.19

I was born to stitch and to use my skills to educate others.

I learned techniques through classes or taught myself. I added my personal style and created award-winning quilts that I could share. I melded my education background and stitching skills and taught others. I achieved the designation of CJ, NQA in order to instruct in a different venue.

During an alternate career in financial management, volunteer hours have been spent exhibiting, teaching, and constructing at the local university, art gallery, and community theater; judging local quilt events; and sharing my collections and skills with interested groups.

I hope I have achieved inspiration, sparked creativity, encouraged, and educated with my art.

AWARDS:
First Place
Innovative Pieced, Amateur
1987

PAUL D. PILGRIM

Paul Pilgrim's quilts reflect his many facets—complex, accomplished, fashionable, entertaining—and are as fresh today as when he made them.

He was about saving the efforts of others, no matter how humble. By incorporating pieces of unfinished projects from the past in his own work, he memorialized many anonymous quiltmakers.

Paul gave license to adopt, improve upon, and complete many unfinished projects that would have eventually been lost forever.

His energy is what is so apparent in his quilts and although he is no longer with us, his spirit, boundless enthusiasm, encouragement, and joy live on through his quilts. His work is still teaching, which, of course, was his passion along with collecting antique quilts.

Gerald Roy

DRESDEN GARDEN
85" x 86", Paul D. Pilgrim, Oakland, CA, 1992. Quilted by Toni Fisher, Belton, MO. Cottons and 1940s' Dresden Plate blocks; hand pieced, hand appliquéd, machine pieced, and hand quilted.
1997.05.17

Yvonne Porcella

My quilts are stories about events, actions, energy, place, past, and future. I invite people to question the thoughts that led to the design:

Appliqué quilts from the 1990s began as a puzzle—pieces fit together to create new design;

Titles spark interest—Waiting for Pink Linoleum, It's All in the Timing, Answering the Riddle.

Quilts in 2000 are abstract—colors, shapes, memories as starting point:

Return to San Juan recalls an award-winning oil painting;

Monkey Sighting color fields reflect quilts from the 1980s;

Bluebirds Fly echoes sentiments from a past fiber art creation.

I ask the viewer to look at my art quilts from a distance to see color and enthusiasm. On closer view, luscious colors side by side create a bold design.

On Wednesday Morning
50" x 70", Yvonne Porcella, Modesto, CA, 1995. Cottons; machine pieced, hand appliquéd and quilted
2001.10.01

FAY PRITTS

Over 25 years ago I learned how to quilt from my grandmother. I find hand quilting relaxing because it gives me time to think and communicate with God. It is also rewarding to see the end results of transforming fabric into a beautiful work of art.

I hope to keep the heritage of quiltmaking alive so that the art of hand quilting will not be lost.

My quilts incorporate traditional techniques while at the same time combining my own contemporary touches. Each quilt truly has a personality of its own, whether it be whimsical, flamboyant, or serious.

As an artist, I hope to pass on the inspiration and knowledge about quiltmaking to start others on this wonderful journey.

WILD ROSE
90" x 90", Fay Pritts, Mt. Pleasant, PA, 1993. Cottons; hand appliquéd and hand quilted.
1996.01.30

AWARDS:
AQS
Best of Show
1994

JULEE PROSE

The thrill of competition and an appreciation for fine detail and precision are at the heart of Julee's quiltmaking.

COMMUNITY BARN RAISING
78" x 105", Julee Prose, Ottumwa, IA, 1987. Cottons; hand appliquéd, machine pieced, and hand quilted. 1997.06.12

AWARDS:
First Place
Theme: Log Cabin
1987

Doris Amiss Rabey

The challenges involved in quilting are what spur Doris's creativity. Learning new techniques or having to improvise her way out of a technical problem give her the sense of achievement and satisfaction.

Feathered Star Bouquet
77" x 77", Doris Amiss Rabey, Hyattsville, MD, 1987. Cottons; hand quilted, pieced, and appliquéd.
1992.03.01

DORIS AMISS RABEY

PRESIDENT'S WREATH VARIATION
72" x 96", Doris Amiss Rabey, Hyattsville, MD, 1986. Cottons and cotton/polyesters; hand appliquéd, machine pieced, and hand quilted.
1997.06.58

AWARDS:
Second Place
Appliqué, Amateur
1986

Sharon Rauba

When I start a quilt, it is because I must explore an idea. I let it take me where it will.

Each quilt is an exciting discovery of possibilities for me—in other words, big girl's play!

Autumn Radiance
81" x 93", Sharon Rauba, Woodridge, IL, 1986. Cottons and cotton blends; hand appliquéd, machine pieced, and hand quilted.
1996.01.03

AWARDS:
AQS
Best of Show
1987

Wendy M. Richardson

Creating nurtures me and is made more special when it connects with the world around me.

It is a joy to celebrate color and pattern and texture, whether to convey a message or simply for the beauty of it.

When it speaks to others—that is the most important achievement of all.

Baskets I
80" x 96", Wendy M. Richardson, Brooklyn Park, MN, 1984. Cottons; machine pieced, hand appliquéd, embroidered, and quilted.
1997.06.04

LUCRETIA ROMEY

Approaching quilting from a painter's point of view allows Lucretia to merge her love of drawing and her passion for artistic expression in the medium of fabric.

CITYSCAPE
50" x 64", Lucretia Romey, East Orleans, MA, 1984. Cottons, cottons blends, and metallic fabrics; hand pieced and hand quilted.
1997.06.10

AWARDS:
First Place
Wall Quilt, Professional
1985

Solveig Ronnqvist

Distant Closeness

75" x 50", Solveig Ronnqvist, Warwick, RI, 1986. Cottons and satins; machine pieced, machine appliquéd, hand appliquéd, and machine quilted. 1997.06.17

Original designs worked up in smaller quilts are Solveig's métier. Foundations of traditional Finnish needlework skills, a class with Jean Ray Laury, and a fashion design degree all reveal themselves in her quilts.

LONNI ROSSI

I am a fiber artist. With fabric and thread, design, color, texture, and form, I strive to tell stories about the possibility of beauty, encouraging the viewer to imagine something out of the realm of their own reality, thus allowing them the opportunity to dream about beautiful things.

Designing and creating fabric—and using those fabrics in my art quilts—is my passion, the thing I cannot possibly be happy without doing.

My art quilts usually involve a back-story, or an interpretation of legend, myth, or history. By allowing the story to become my momentary reality, my imagination takes me to another place, another time, another life.

My hope is that my fabrics and art quilts do that for the people who view them.

AWARDS:
RJR Best Wall Quilt
1999

CABINS IN THE COSMOS
50" x 55", Lonni Rossi, Wynnewood, PA, 1998. Commercial, hand-dyed, surface designed cottons; gold lamé, computer chips, aviation artifact; machine pieced, quilted, and stitched; and fused.
1999.03.01

ADRIEN ROTHSCHILD

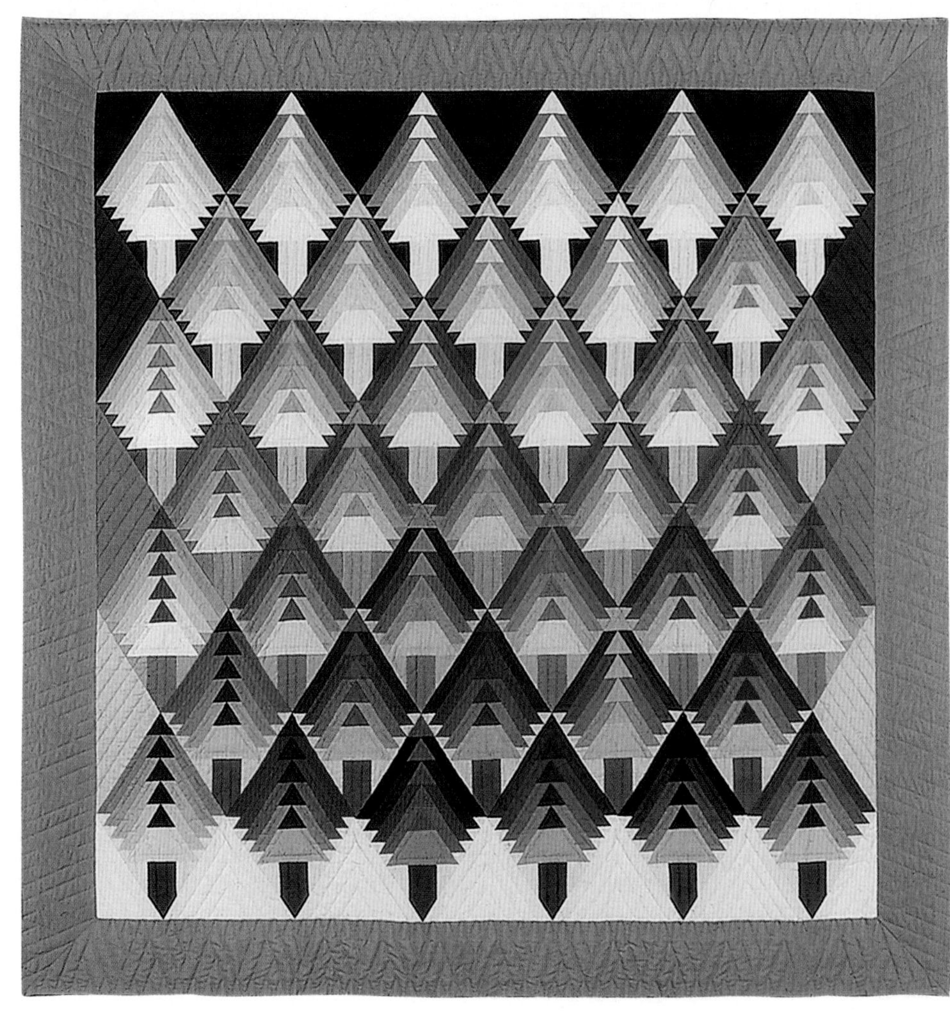

Art, mechanics, organics, and quilting professionally describe Adrien's achievements.

DESIGNER CHRISTMAS TREES
62" x 62", Adrien Rothschild, Baltimore, MD, 1990. Hand-dyed cottons; machine pieced and hand quilted.
1991.03.01

AWARDS:
Second Place
Wall Quilt, Amateur
1991

Gerald E. Roy

My quilts, like my paintings, are personal expressions I am compelled to create for my own well being. I am pleased when others can relate to them, but creating "ART" is the furthest thing from my mind. I am doing what I have to do and what I have been trained to do in order to satisfy and feel accomplished.

As we evolve so does the work. The joy is when someone else can relate to your experiences and react to the work because it triggers some personal response in them.

To respect and honor the inherent abilities of the medium and use it to its best advantage is the key.

Complimentary Composition
65" x 63", Gerald Roy, Warner, NH, 1998/1999. Cottons; hand appliquéd, machine assembled; hand quilted by Toni Fisher.
2004.04.01

LINDA M. ROY

Spice of Life
82" x 82", Linda M. Roy, Pittsfield, MA, 2003. Cottons; metallic thread and perle cotton embroidery; ruching, machine pieced, hand appliquéd and quilted.
2004.01.01

My joy in quiltmaking is to make something lasting that reflects my inner person.

My hopes are that my quilts bring the viewer a moment of reflection and feelings of peace and contentment, if only for a few minutes.

I consider most of my quilts "heirloom," and hope they are around for generations for my family to enjoy on a bed or on a wall.

I find it enjoyable savoring and not rushing the design or handwork, taking the time to find a way to get each design from my mind and sketched onto graph paper and then sewn into the fabrics.

My quilts are definitely not quickly made, and I hope they reflect the love and patience it took to complete each one.

AWARDS:
Hancock's of Paducah
Best of Show
2004

MARGARET RUDD

In her lifetime, Margaret went from making the utilitarian quilts of rural Kentucky to producing more contemporary work to sharing her skills and vision with young quilters.

SOPHISTICATION
55½" x 55½", Margaret Rudd, Cadiz, KY, 1987, designed by Ross Tucker, Corydon, IN. Cottons, silk, suede cloth; machine pieced and hand quilted.
1993.02.01

LINDA KAREL SAGE

In my quiltmaking I hope to gladden the heart of the viewer with color, pattern, and texture.

I want my quilts to be fun for the viewer.

BROWN COUNTY LOG CABINS
87" x 93", Linda Karel Sage, Morgantown, IN, 1985. Cottons, cotton blends; machine pieced and hand quilted.
1997.06.08

AWARDS:
First Place
Traditional Patchwork, Amateur
1986

LINDA KAREL SAGE

INDIANA CRAZY
70" x 71", Linda Karel Sage, Morgantown, IN, 1988. Cottons and blends; machine and hand pieced; hand appliquéd, painted, embroidered, tied, and quilted.
1997.06.30

Priscilla Sage

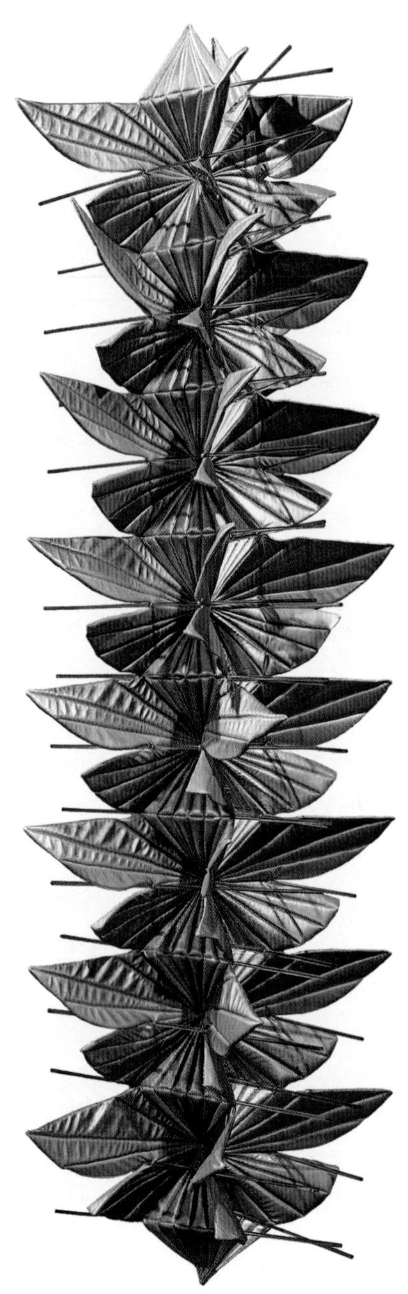

"In my work, the form comes first," says Priscilla Sage. "I start with small, white paper models to examine an idea and to work out the geometry of a piece. The beauty of paper models is that you can play and play and, if necessary, crumple them up and start anew. It is hard to leave this stage, but eventually it's time to construct a full-size paper model to check the calculations, the connections, and the tension. I also design for the slivers of space that create important tension between forms, and for the openings to interior spaces that offer surprises. When the form is clean, it's time for color.

"Although I work on a large scale, my inspiration comes from the structure of natural forms that can be as small as mosses, as sinuous as the DNA helix, as vast as images from the Hubble telescope, or as personal as the human body."

Priscilla's sculptures are padded with car headliner about one fourth inch in. This is felted on one side and polyurethane on the other. Look at the ceiling of your car and you can see what this is like.

Winged Vermillion
60" x 16" x 14", Priscilla Sage, Ames, Iowa, 2011. Silver Mylar polyester, acrylic paint, acrylic rods, Japanese paper, car headliner; machine and hand stitched
2013.01.01

Lyn Peare Sandberg

What I hope to achieve with my artistry is such a hard question for an artist, as artistry isn't that linear. What we achieve with it is in the life of the piece and the reactions to it after it leaves our studio.

What I hoped to achieve (motivation?) was a chronicle of a time and place born of my personal history—single and sailing free in another medium, the ocean—the illusive atmosphere and freedom that time allowed me to experience, before marriage, children, and methodical living.

So I'd have to answer that I hope to achieve sharing my freedom through the trespass of art.

AWARDS:

3rd Place

Innovative Pieced, Professional

1989

Boat in a Bottle Sampler

80" x 92", Lyn Peare Sandberg, Capitola, CA, 1988. Cottons; machine pieced and hand quilted.

1992.09.01

Rose Sanders

Tradition, authenticity, quality, and precision define the artistry and achievement Rose seeks in her quiltmaking.

Crown of Cerise
94" x 94", Rose Sanders, Harahan, LA, 1986. Cottons; hand appliquéd and hand quilted with trapunto. National Quilting Association Masterpiece Quilt.
1997.07.05

JANE SASSAMAN

Jane celebrates the energy and beauty of nature, especially plant life, in her work. She teaches others to nurture creativity, observe more closely, and how to overcome creative obstacles.

TREE OF LIFE: SPRING
69½" x 78½", Jane Sassaman, Harvard, IL, 1994. Cottons; machine appliquéd, pieced, and quilted.
2007.02.01

AWARDS:
1st Place
Wall Quilt, Professional
1995

SHARON SCHAMBER

Being true to herself and listening to her creative soul guides Sharon's quiltmaking. She considers herself a teacher first, then a quiltmaker.

FLOWER OF LIFE
87" x 87", Sharon Schamber, Payson, AZ, 2007. Cottons; machine pieced and appliquéd, longarm machine quilted.
2007.05.01

AWARDS:
Hancock's of Paducah
Best of Show
2007

SHARON SCHAMBER

SEDONA ROSE
105" x 110", Sharon Schamber, Payson, AZ, 2006. Cottons, Swarovski® crystals; machine pieced and appliquéd, longarm machine quilted.
2006.03.01

AWARDS:
Hancock's of Paducah
Best of Show
2006

ELSIE SCHLABACH

Elsie draws on family and cultural influences when making her quilts. Color, pattern scale, and quilting design combine to make her quilts successful.

AMISH MUTUAL AID
75" x 83", Elsie Schlabach, Millersburg, OH, 1993. Cottons; machine pieced, hand pieced, and hand quilted.
1997.07.01

Cynthia Schmitz

Machine quilting combines with color, fabric, sewing, and problem solving in Cynthia's quilts.

Blueberry Morning
85" x 85", Cynthia Schmitz,
Arlington Heights, IL, 2002.
Cottons, monofilament nylon thread; machine pieced, trapuntoed, and machine quilted.
2003.02.01

AWARDS:
Bernina
Machine Workmanship
2003

ELAINE M. SEAMAN

I know people do connect with my quilts, but I can't say why.

I like to think it's because I haven't strayed too far from tradition. I'm a use-what-you-have, create-from-scraps, repeated-geometric-pattern kind of quilter.

Like legions of women before me, I like the challenge, the structure, the utility, and the artistry of quiltmaking.

I love to see the delight in the eyes of others as they view my work. Each new quilt is tangible evidence that I am content doing what I do, which, I assume, is the goal of every artist.

PROSPERITY
84" x 84", Elaine M. Seaman, Kalamazoo, MI, 1985. Cottons; hand pieced, machine pieced, and hand quilted.
1997.06.59

CHERYL L. SEE

STAR STRUCK
91" x 80", Cheryl L. See, Ashburn, VA, 2011. Cottons, perle cotton, embroidery floss, cotton and silk threads, glass and plastic beads, 50/50 bamboo/cotton batting, Hobbs Heirloom Premium 80% Cotton/20% Polyester batting; hand pieced, hand appliquéd, hand beaded, hand quilted.
2012.02.02

AWARDS:
AQS Hand Workmanship
2012

I never liked history in school, but history on quilts and their makers fascinates me. There is always a story of why someone chose to make the quilt, the materials they used, techniques and of course whom the intended recipient of the quilt was to be. For me, my quilts are a way to be remembered by on this Earth when I am no longer here as I have no children to continue my memory.

STAR STRUCK took me three and a half years to complete. The design evolved with time. I had made a traditional hexagon quilt before in a Mary Washington pattern by hand and even though it took forever, I loved the handwork. I wanted to design a quilt with hexagons that didn't look like a traditional hexagon quilt. I decided to use colors in a rainbow. My stepfather had just died two weeks before and the family had seen many beautiful rainbows that had meant a lot to us and I believe that is why I was thinking in rainbow colors."

JUDY HENDRY SEIDEL

HEARTS & STARS
40" x 48", Judy Hendry Seidel, Ft. Collins, CO, 1984. Cottons and cotton blends; hand and machine pieced, hand quilted.
1997.06.28

I don't make quilts for art's sake; I do make them for heart's sake.

I selfishly achieve great satisfaction from designing quilts, choosing fabric, playing with it, hand quilting it, and seeing how the quilt turns out.

I don't know if I'm scattered or eclectic, but I get my inspiration from many directions. My greatest achievement occurs when a person turns up who loves one of my quilts and then it becomes theirs.

I'm a person who would be making quilts no matter where I happened to be or what might be going on around me—I make quilts because I can't help but do so. They give me great joy and I have the feeling that others delight in them also.

AUDREE L. SELLS

My ultimate hope is that others will feel joy and be inspired when viewing my quilts.

Since making JAVANESE JUNGLE in 1988 I've had many opportunities to work with quilters of all skill levels. It has been a rewarding journey sharing my ideas and methods in the hopes of enhancing their enthusiasm for quilts and art in general.

For me, quilting is more than a hobby. It is something I do every day—often all day. It is my passion.

I wish for everyone a passion of that degree in their lives.

When showing my art quilts in public venues, classes, and programs, my goal is always to bring pleasure and inspiration to the viewer.

AWARDS:
First Place
Appliqué, Amateur
1988

JAVANESE JUNGLE
75" x 94", Audree L. Sells, Chaska, MN, 1988. Cottons; hand pieced, hand appliquéd, hand embroidered and beaded, and hand quilted.
1992.16.01

Polly Sepulvado

Grandmother's Engagement Ring
76" x 94", Polly Sepulvado, M.D., Vicksburg, MS, 1986. Cottons; hand appliquéd, machine pieced, and hand quilted.
1997.06.27

I continue to be passionate about quilting after 32 years.

I work full-time but make time to quilt "a little" every day. I have the luxury of a large quilt room and can walk away and leave a project at any point and return whenever I can. Usually there are more than a dozen projects going at once.

I'm enthusiastic about learning new techniques and styles. Although I have challenged myself to make wallhangings, I really like making bed quilts. They are used by my family and I enjoy displaying my quilts at my office.

I suppose what I want to accomplish with my quilt artistry is to satisfy my own creative desires and to try to please others with my work.

Awards:
Third Place
Traditional Pieced, Amateur
1986

JONATHON SHANNON

Pragmatism and a passing fancy with quiltmaking have defined Jonathan's artistry.

AIR SHOW
81" x 81", Jonathan Shannon, Phoenix, AZ, 1992. Cottons; machine pieced, hand appliquéd, couched cording, and hand quilted. Named one of the 100 Best American Quilts of the 20th Century.
1996.01.01

AWARDS:
AQS
Best of Show
1993

MARION SHENK

A lifetime of quilting has been a seamless artistic experience for Marion.

SHADOW BALTIMORE BRIDE
86" x 102", Marion Shenk, Scottdale, PA, 1986. Cotton broadcloth, voile, and cotton embroidery floss; hand quilted by various quilters at maker's quilt shop.
1997.06.70

AWARDS:
Third Place
Other Techniques, Professional
1986

Mark Sherman

"For me the most difficult thing about quilt making is coming up with an idea," says Mark Sherman. "In this case the idea came from my wife Sherry, who is neither a quilter nor an artist. She is a talented physician but she will be the first to acknowledge that sewing is not her forte."

The design for WISTERIA is from a stained glass window by Louis Comfort Tiffany titled "Snowball and Wisteria" circa 1907. Mark first drew the design on small paper then had copies made that were the actual size of the quilt. He then made all the appliqué pieces, searching hand-dyed fabric for just the right colors and turning the edges under as perfectly as possible. Once all the appliqué pieces were made, he machine appliquéd them to the black background.

"Quilting for me is a road," Mark says. "One filled with many choices and many ways to achieve a goal. Quilting has shown me how much my family loves me and wants only the best for me. It's just like life. Thank God for quilting and quilters."

WISTERIA
58½" x 84", Mark Sherman, Coral Springs, FL, 2008. Hand-dyed, -stained, and –painted cottons; machine pieced, machine appliquéd, and longarm machine quilted
2009.04.01

VIRGINIA SICILIANO

Traditional patterns used in unusual ways, color, fabric selection and use, and hand quilting are the challenges Virginia finds most exciting and satisfying in quiltmaking.

SAMARKAND
80½" x 81", Virginia Siciliano, Lebanon, PA, 2001. Cottons; machine pieced, hand quilted.
2007.11.01

AWARDS:
Third Place
Traditional Pieced, Amateur
2001

JUDY SIMMONS

The drive to become a fiber artist was greatly influenced by my family who made everything with their sewing machines.

I work intuitively, pulling inspiration from the things I love such as old family pictures and papers, textured rocks, peeling paint and crumbling stones on sidewalks and buildings, things that have endured the elements of time, interesting but not necessarily beautiful. I am also inspired by the beautiful colors and textures of nature.

My camera is always with me, ready to capture these wonderful things. This imagery is printed, embellished, and combined with other surface design techniques to create a unique piece.

NOSEGAY
36" diameter, Judy Simmons, Marietta, GA, 1986. Cottons; hand appliquéd (including broderie perse) and hand quilted.
1997.06.47

MARTHA B. SKELTON

Before she passed away, Martha was one of America's best-known quilters. She is remembered by friends as a teacher and mentor for those in the craft.

CHIPS AND WHETSTONES
80" x 89½", Martha B. Skelton, Vicksburg, MS, 1987. Cottons; hand and machine pieced, hand appliquéd, and hand quilted.
1992.02.01

MARTHA B. SKELTON

NEW YORK BEAUTY
77" x 90", Martha B. Skelton, Vicksburg, MS, 1986. Cottons; hand pieced, machine pieced, and hand quilted.
1997.06.44

AWARDS:
First Place
Tradtional Pieced, Professional
1987

Ruth Britton Smalley

Ruth's lifelong involvement in several art forms, including painting, sculpture, and jewelry making, built the foundation for her quiltmaking.

Square within a Square within a Square within a Square

102" x 102", Ruth Britton Smalley, Houston, TX, 1986. Cottons; machine pieced and hand quilted.
1997.08.01

Awards:
Third Place
Theme: Log Cabin
1987

Fraser Smith

I make trompe l'oeil wood sculptures of items made of fabric or leather. My subject matter is drawn from things that we tend to save or cherish even after they are no longer useful—items we might want to keep simply for the memories they hold.

Like all trompe l'oeil artists, I'm trying to challenge the viewer, but I want to take it beyond the simple mastery of technique.

In my quilt works, I'm attempting to combine good design and color use with an interesting but unexpected object.

I want the viewer to initially feel that it's a bit "out of place." I want them to think, "Well, that's interesting, but why is it there?" When they discover it's wood, they have to reevaluate.

Floating

65" x 42" x 4", is a solid wood sculpture by Fraser Smith, Tampa, FL. Appearing to be softly draped over a rope, the folds of Fraser's hanging quilt fool the eye. Tiny indentations mimic quilting stitches, but at more than 80 pounds this carved solid wood sculpture is anything but wrap-around cuddly.

LOIS T. SMITH

SPRINGTIME SAMPLER
108" x 108," Lois T. Smith, Rockville, MD, 1986. Cottons, rayon thread; machine pieced and machine quilted.
1997.06.72

Since the very first day of my quiltmaking journey, I have been passionately devoted to teaching the art of creativity and originality in quiltmaking and to making quilts that reflect my deepest feelings and record my most precious memories.

In this endeavor I have strayed from the historic path and played with nontraditional materials and techniques.

My goal has been to help students develop a basic foundation of skills that they can adapt and use as they pursue their individual artistic goals.

When skill and artistic energy ignite, the world is a more beautiful place.

AWARDS:
Third Place
Traditional Pieced,
Professional
1986

NANCY ANN SOBEL

I hope to inspire others to become confident and respectful of their own personal artistic vision.

I also hope to leave a legacy to my future generations that artistry is a wonderful gift and to "Be sure that each one is doing his very best, for then he will have the personal satisfaction of work well done, and won't need to compare himself with someone else." (Galatians 6:4).

Let the work of your hands be guided by what is in your mind and heart.

AWARDS:
AQS
Best of Show
1991

DAWN SPLENDOR
94" x 94", Nancy Ann Sobel, Brooktondale, NY, 1991. Cottons; machine pieced, hand appliquéd, and hand quilted.
1996.01.08

Nancy Ann Sobel

A Midwinter Night's Dream
99" x 99", Nancy Ann Sobel, Brooktondale, NY, 1988. Cottons; machine pieced, hand appliquéd, and hand quilted. 1996.01.17

Awards:
Gingher
Hand Workmanship
1990

JUDY SOGN

Quiltmaking in all its forms, including appreciating the work of others, is at the heart of Judy's approach to her art.

STARBURST
95" x 95", Judy Sogn, Seattle, WA, 1990. Cottons, over-dyed cottons; machine pieced and hand quilted.
1997.06.75

AWARDS:
Second Place
Traditional Pieced, Professional
1991

MILDRED SORRELLS

CHARISMA

84" x 84", Mildred Sorrells, Macomb, IL, 2010. Cottons; YLI silk thread, Aurifil cotton thread, Superior King Tut thread; Hobbs wool batt; machine pieced, machine appliquéd, machine quilted.
2010.04.01

"I love everything about quilting," writes Mildred Sorrells. "I like hand work as well as machine work and try to add a little something different in each quilt. I love working with colors and trying to create my own designs. I don't want to use anyone else's pattern, but I get my ideas from all kinds of things, antique quilts, Dover books, quilt books, etc. When I am making a quilt I usually draw out some kind of a plan but will probably change it as I go along.

"In quilting there is a place for everyone, whether you like to just piece or appliqué by hand or machine, ...hand quilt or machine quilt with a regular machine or a longarm, art quilts, or whatever you want to do. Since I started quilting in 1981 I have tried just about every technique.

"My quilts are more traditional and I like the challenge of entering my quilts in contests."

AWARDS:

Bernina
Machine Workmanship
2010

Collection of The National Quilt Museum

Patricia Spadaro

I enjoy quilting because it is a fulfilling part of my life, and I find it very relaxing.

I am fearful that it is becoming a lost art, as young people become more involved in technology and less involved in handmade crafts.

I hope that the care I put into my quilting, including my intricate stitching and handmade wax thread, will inspire others to take the time to learn this art and take pride in it.

Quilted Counterpane
72" x 100", Patricia Spadaro, Delmar, NY, 1985. Polished cotton; hand quilted.
1997.06.60

AWARDS:
Second Place
Other Techniques, Amateur
1986

DOREEN SPECKMANN

Innovation, creativity, and humor infused every aspect of Doreen's life, including her quilts.

THE BLADE
62" x 84", Doreen Speckmann, Madison, WI, 1985. Cottons; machine pieced, hand quilted.
1997.06.06

AWARDS:
First Place
Patchwork, Professional
1985

Louise Stafford

Early in her life, quilts were but a necessary chore for Louise. Later, they became fun, and a way to reveal her playful nature.

Colonial Lady
86" x 99½", Louise Stafford, Brewerton, WA, 1984. Cotton and cotton blends; hand pieced, hand appliquéd, hand embroidered, and hand quilted.
1997.07.04

LOUISE STAFFORD

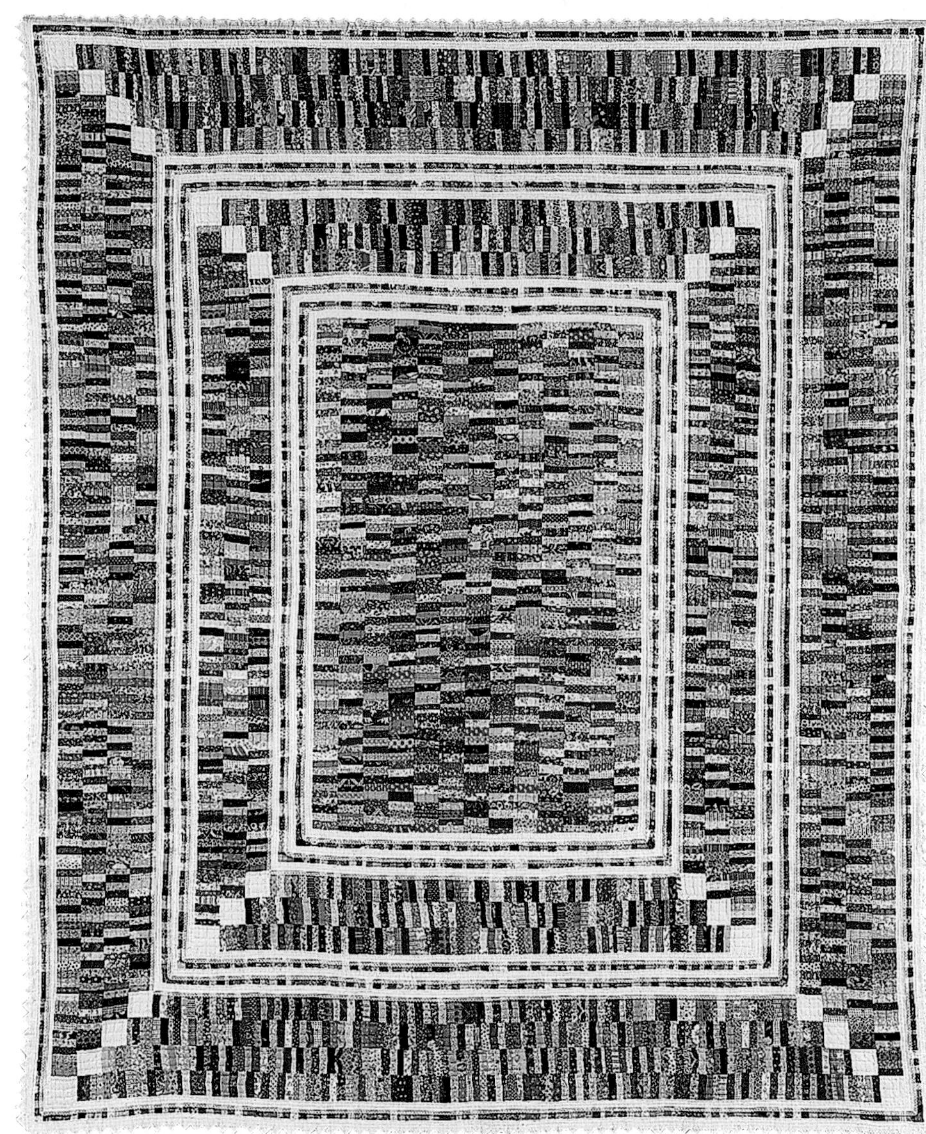

WASTE NOT, WANT NOT
79" x 91", Louise Stafford, Bremerton, WA, 1990. Cottons, cotton blends, lace; machine pieced and hand quilted.
1992.04.01

AILEEN STANNIS

The combined satisfactions of meticulous hand workmanship and finishing a quilt give Aileen her sense of artistry and achievement.

BALTIMORE REMEMBERED
83" x 103", Aileen Stannis, Berkley, MI, 1996. Cottons; hand appliquéd, hand pieced, and hand quilted.
1996.03.01

AWARDS:
Gingher
Hand Workmanship
1996

Arlene Statz

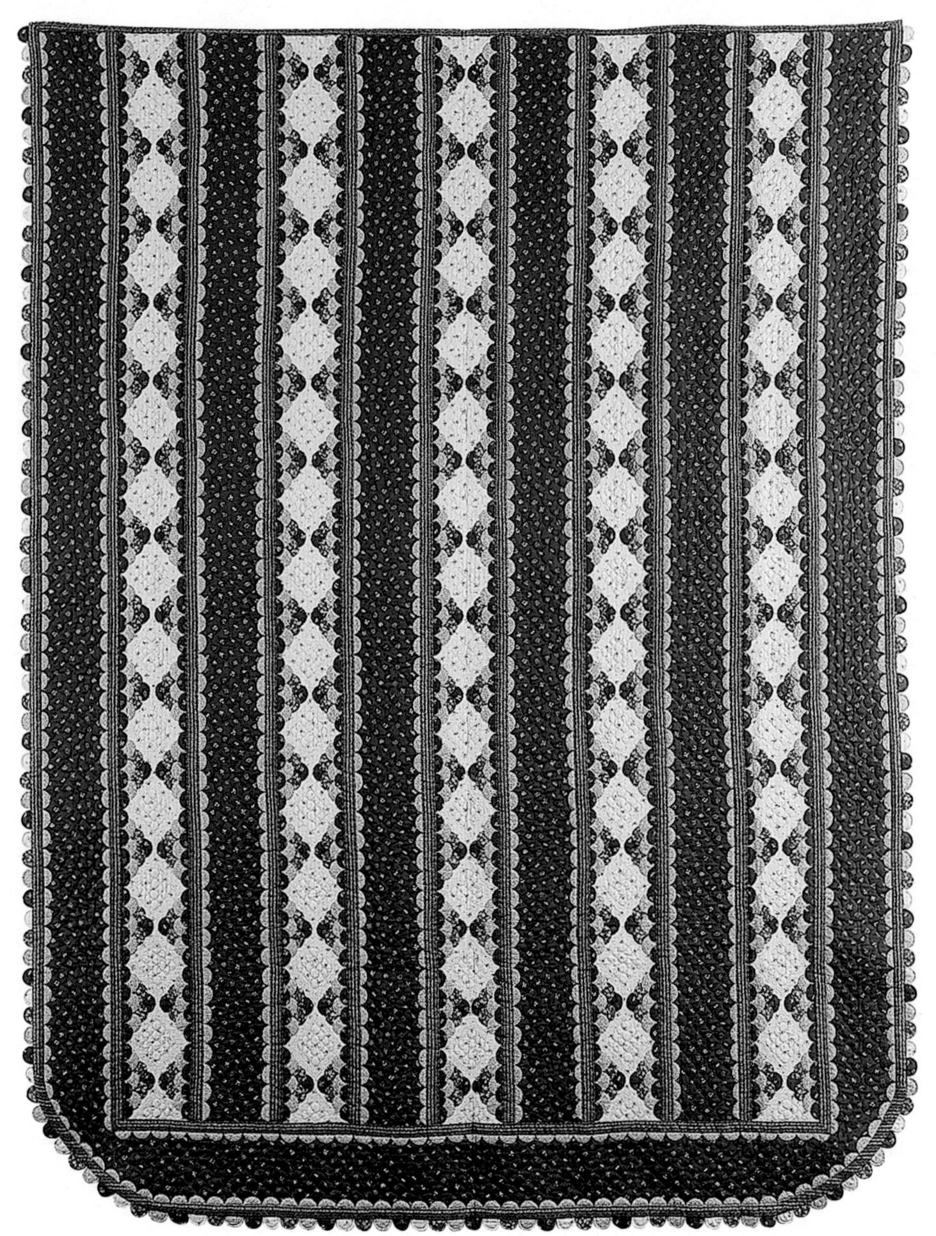

While she was alive, having two quilts in The National Quilt Museum (then MAQS) was a source of pride and joy for Arlene.

Clamshell
84" x 104", Arlene Statz, Sun Prairie, WI, 1984. Cottons; hand appliquéd, machine pieced, and hand quilted. 1997.06.11

ARLENE STATZ

GRANDMOTHER'S ENGAGEMENT RING
74" x 96", Arlene Statz, Sun Prairie, WI, 1986. Cottons; machine pieced, hand appliquéd, and hand quilted.
1997.06.26

Carole Steiner

The primary value of quilting for Carole is how quilting brings women together in a sisterhood.

Lilies Are Forever
76" x 88", Carole Steiner, Santa Maria, CA, 1994. Cottons; machine pieced, hand appliquéd, and hand quilted.
1996.01.15

Awards:
Gingher
Hand Workmanship
1995

JOYCE STEWART

Faith, color, and devotion to her sister have framed Joyce's quilting achievements.

CELEBRATION
46" x 46", Joyce Stewart, Rexburg, ID, 1988. Cotton; machine pieced and machine quilted.
1992.11.01

JOYCE STEWART

SPLENDOR OF THE RAJAHS
84" x 106", Joyce Stewart, Rexburg, ID, 1985. Cottons; machine pieced and hand quilted. Pattern from Curves Unlimited by Joyce M. Schlotzhauer.
1997.06.71

SUSAN STEWART

This quilt was conceived with the thought that if I made a gray quilt, the fur from my two gray cats wouldn't show! To make a gray quilt not drab, I wanted to use reflective fabric and threads, and lots of texture to make it look like hammered silver. I used digitized machine embroidery in a way that was integral to the design of the quilt. The digitized machine embroidery designs from Zundt Designs were carefully positioned and stitched on the whole-cloth background, cross-hatched double-needle pintucked fabric was appliquéd, and the spines for the feathers were stitched with decorative machine stitching. After free-motion quilting, the windows in the central circle were cut out and faced, and the free-standing lace inserts were attached.

AWARDS:

First Place, Bed Quilt, Home Machine Quilted
2011

EVERY CLOUD HAS A SILVER LINING
85" x 85", Susan Stewart, Pittsburg, KS, 2010. Silk/cotton blend, cotton; poly, metallic and monofilament threads; wool batt; digitized machine embroidery from Zundt Designs, machine quilted.
2011.04.01

SUSAN STEWART

RADIANCE

75" x 74", Susan Stewart, Pittsburg, KS, 2011. Hand-dyed Cherrywood cottons, Robert Kaufman silk/cotton "Radiance" fabric (hence the name of the quilt!), Hobbs Tuscany wool batt, Isacord and Superior polyester machine embroidery threads, YLI metallic thread, YLI nylon monofilament thread; Superior Threads silk Kimono #100, polyester So Fine, and polyester The Bottom Line threads; embroidery designs by Zundt Design; machine pieced, digitized machine embroidered, free-standing lace made on water-soluble stabilizer, decorative machine stitched, free-motion hand-guided quilted, hand-appliquéd facing.
2012.02.03

How long did it take to make this quilt? I like to tell people who ask this question that it took me 50 years to develop the skills to make it, and 6 to 8 months to construct it!

The triangular machine embroidery design in the diamond star points was the inspiration for the entire quilt, as well as the determining factor for the size of the star points, the size of the small pieces diamonds making up the star points, and the size of the strips between the star points. I wanted to develop the secondary pattern created by the embroidery over the pieced top. The colors used for the embroidery were all inspired by the gradated pack of Cherrywood fabrics.

AWARDS:
Bernina
Machine Workmanship
2012

SUSAN STEWART

"Fabric and thread have been my passion since I began sewing at age five," writes Susan Stewart. "After working as an heirloom sewing designer and author for 16 years, I began quilting in 2004. My love of lace and delicate details works its way into my quilts. I often include digitized machine embroidery in my quilts, and strive to make the embroidery an integral part of the design."

TULIP FIRE
70" x 70", Susan Stewart, Pittsburg, KS, 2012. Silk/cotton blend fabric, wool batting, cotton backing; polyester, metallic, and cotton (bobbin only) machine embroidery threads; nylon monofilament, silk, and polyester quilting thread; machine embroidery designs from Zundt Design; machine foundation pieced, machine embroidered, double-needle pintucked, shaped lace insertion, decorative machine stitched, free-motion machine quilted.
2013.06.03

AWARDS:
Bernina
Machine Workmanship
2013

Susan Gloria
STEWART & MEYER

GLORIA'S GARDEN
73" x 73", Susan Stewart and Gloria Meyer, Pittsburg, KS, 2009. Cottons; cotton, polyester, and metallic threads; wool batt; machine pieced, machine embroidered lace, table-set longarm machine quilted.
2010.05.01

This quilt is a collaboration between daughter Susan Stewart and mother Gloria Meyer. Gloria chose the fabrics and pieced the quilt and Susan did all the digitized machine embroidery and quilting. The piecing is a variation of the "Blooming Nine Patch" pattern from *Tradition with a Twist: Variations on Your Favorite Quilts* by Blanche Young and Dalene Young Stone (C&T Publishing, Inc., 1996). The machine embroidery designs are from Zundt Designs and OESD. "It was very special for me to be able to share the excitement of winning this award with my mother," writes Susan.

"This is the first contest I have ever entered and was completely surprised in winning such a prestigious award," writes Gloria.

AWARDS:
Gammill Longarm Machine Quilting
2010

Heide Stoll-Weber

"I had started dyeing fabric professionally in 1994 and just managed to make a living from selling my fabrics," writes Heide Stoll-Weber. "At that time I only allowed myself relatively small amounts to keep for my own artistic purposes. But – a little bit of everything can end up being quite a lot, too. So I ended up with all these strips of different width of a new batch of poplin that dyed beautifully. It was so wonderfully overwhelming to work with these that this particular piece almost made itself effortlessly on my workwall."

Forest Fire
49¼" x 81", Heidi Stoll-Weber, Frankfurt Main, Germany, 1997. Cottons, hand-dyed by the artist; machine pieced, machine quilted.
2010.02.01

Frances Stone

I learned how to piece a Nine Patch when I was nine, but didn't take up quilting in earnest until an accident left me in a full body cast.

I am no longer able to do much quilting, especially on large quilts, due to bad eyesight and arthritis in my hands and back, but I still try to make baby quilts for the young mothers at my work and church for their new babies.

Peace and Love
96" x 92", Frances Stone, Mayfield, KY, 1985. Cottons, lace, and ribbon; shadow appliqué, hand quilted with embroidery thread.
1997.06.54

JANET STONE

Realizing she had almost a complete alphabet of brass charms led Janet to create CHARM SCHOOL, her eleventh alphabet quilt. Each letter is raw-edge appliquéd, framed, and attached to a small square of heavy pellon, which is riveted to the quilt. The 26-appliqué blocks of varying sizes, set between the narrow black and white sashing, are decorated with hot-fixed jewels, pearls, and rhinestuds as well as a letter and the charm representing that letter. The quilt is heavily and beautifully custom quilted in varying patterns including florals, pebbles, straight-line outline, curved outline, and crosshatch. A tiny metallic cord is couched by hand just inside the binding with small lime green, purple, and turquiose accents as the perfect counterpoint to the primarily beige and black color scheme.

AWARDS:

Moda

Best Wall Quilt

2013

CHARM SCHOOL

49" x 74", Janet Stone, Overland Park, KS, 2012. Cottons, brass charms, interfacing, cording; machine pieced, machine appliquéd, hand couched, machine quilted.

2013.06.04

ELAINE STONEBRAKER

The dimension achievable in quiltmaking is the source of Elaine's sense of artistry.

RISING MOONS
73" x 67", Elaine Stonebraker, Scottsdale, AZ, 1988. Cottons; hand pieced and hand quilted. 1997.06.64

AWARDS:
Second Place
Pictorial Wall Quilt
1989

Dorothy Mackley STOVALL

The quality Dorthy seeks in her quiltmaking comes to her better via handwork than machine work.

Star Bright
81" x 96", Dorothy Mackley Stovall, Livingston, MT, 1985. Cottons; hand pieced and hand quilted.
1997.06.74

JANICE STREETER

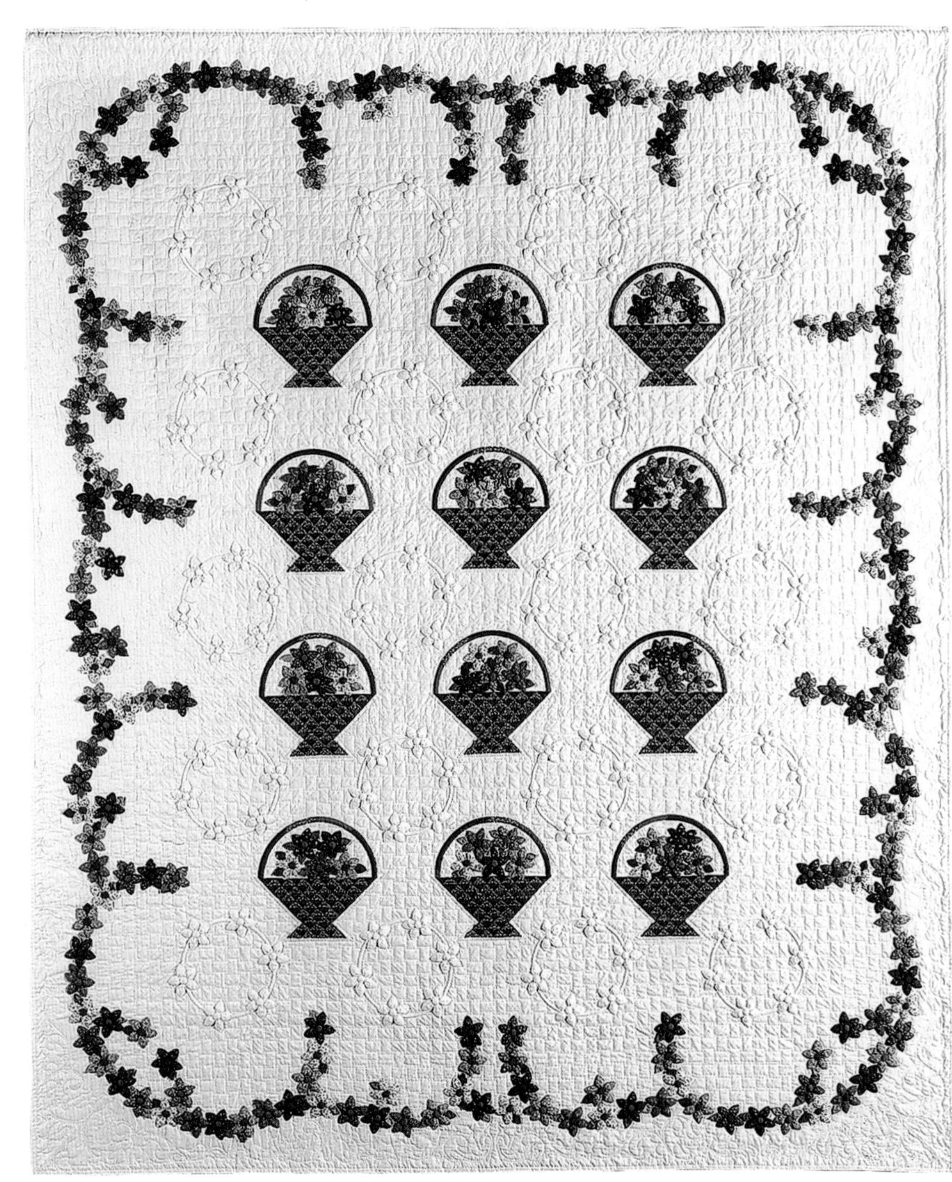

Expressing her individuality is at the core of Janice's quilt-making artistry and achievement.

SPRING FLOWER BASKET
88" x 103", Janice Streeter, Virginia Beach, VA, 1989. Cottons; machine pieced, hand appliquéd, and hand quilted. National Quilting Association Masterpiece Quilt.
1996.01.23

AWARDS:
Gingher
Hand Workmanship
1989

KARMEN STRENG

I retired from serious quilting many years ago. I attend quilt conferences several times a year and enjoy seeing the work others are doing and visiting with old friends.

I produce five or six quilts per year. These I give to children, grandchildren, friends, and charity.

I love my hobby. The challenges keep me involved and vital.

CELEBRATION OF AUTUMN
86" x 86", Karmen Streng, Davis, CA, 1985. Cottons; machine pieced and hand quilted.
1992.18.01

AWARDS:

Second Place

Innovative Pieced, Amateur

1986

MARIE STURMER

Marie's approach to quilt-making comes from her formal art training and then a lifetime of teaching art, which required her to adapt many artistic skills and techniques. Painted stencil quilts are her trademark.

RIBBONS AND ROSES
72" x 86", Marie Sturmer, Traverse City, MI, 1989. Cotton; stenciled, hand embroidered, and hand quilted.
1997.06.63

PATRICIA L. STYRING

Being prolific, having fun with color, entering shows, and seeing her sense of humor evidenced in fabric are the basic tenets of quiltmaking achievement for Patricia.

PETROGLYPH
66" x 79", Patricia L. Styring, St. Augustine, FL, 1997. Cottons, metallic acrylic paint, fabric paint, bleach discharge; machine pieced, appliquéd, and quilted.
2006.01.01

AWARDS:
First Place
Mixed Techniques, Professional
1998

Eileen Bahring Sullivan

The precision in Eileen's work comes from technique. The designs and colors come from nature. She believes that there is an artist inside each one of us.

When Grandmother's Lily Garden Blooms

62" x 82", Eileen Bahring Sullivan, Alpharetta, GA, 1990. Cottons and blends, hand-dyed fabrics; machine pieced, hand embroidered, and hand quilted.
1997.06.91

Awards:
First Place
Innovative Pieced, Professional
1990

SHERRY SUNDAY

Teaching and designing give Sherry a distinct sense of accomplishment in her quiltmaking.

INDIAN SUMMER
106" x 106," Sherry Sunday, New Kingston, PA, 1993. Cottons; machine pieced, appliquéd, and quilted. 1997.07.13

GABRIELLE SWAIN

TOTEM
62" x 50", Gabrielle Swain, Watauga, TX, 2003. Cottons; machine pieced, hand appliquéd, hand embroidered, and hand quilted.
2003.04.01

AWARDS:
RJR
Best Wall Quilt
2003

As an artist working in a variety of media, when I discovered quiltmaking, all my needs were satisfied. Painting, photography, and graphic design all seemed a perfect fit for quilts.

After going through many stages, appliqué became my favorite technique. With this technique, almost any design could be accomplished.

Since that time, the majority of my work is centered on nature. Believing in the principle of working from where you live, almost all my work is inspired by the landscapes in Texas.

Celebrating nature as a part of who we are in instead of separate from us will continue to be the focus of my work.

Hopefully, the work will do justice to the beauty outside my door.

Collection of The National Quilt Museum

MYRL LEHMAN TAPUNGOT

I have always had an over-active imagination, and early on realized that I would never have enough time in one lifetime to see all of the designs I dreamed up completed.

In 1979 after my husband retired from the US Navy, we retired to the island of Mindanao in the Philippines. Mindanaoans are very clever and talented, and in the years since our arrival we have been able to train over 400 people in making some of the most beautiful quilts imaginable.

LE JARDIN DE NOS REVES (MY GARDEN OF DREAMS)
68" x 88", Myrl Lehman Tapungot, Cagayan de Oro, Philippines, 1997. Cottons; hand quilted with trapunto and hand embroidered and beaded.
1997.01.01

AWARDS:
Gingher
Hand Workmanship
1997

Carol Taylor

Revolutions
47½" x 55", Carol Taylor, Pittsford, NY, 2002. Cotton sateen, wool batting, rayon thread; machine pieced, machine quilted.
2010.08.01

Revolutions is part of Carol Taylor's Gong Series. "This quilt is about taking a motif and rotating it," says Carol. "How many revolutions does it take to make a circle or to create an entire composition?"

The gong motif is Carol's design that is basically a quarter circle with crossbars that looks rather like Chinese chopsticks. By combining this motif in various ways, she has come up with a whole series of quilts. When the motif is used as a whole circle, it suggests a Chinese gong in an oriental housing. By using values in different ways, this series has evolved into 39 quilts, including Revolutions.

Internationally known, Carol Taylor is an award-winning artist who approaches her quilt making with intensity and seemingly boundless energy. She is a teacher by degree, outgoing by nature, and her workshops are said to be "fun, motivational, and non-threatening."

Deborah Warren TECHENTIN

A lifelong fascination with all things needle and thread led up to Deborah's passion for making quilts.

MARINER'S COMPASS
78" x 90", Deborah Warren Techentin, Kalamazoo, MI, 1985. Cottons; machine and hand pieced and hand quilted.
1997.06.38

Barbara Temple

Barbara has preferred making picture quilts from the start of her quilting life, likening the process of creating depth and dimension in fabric to painting.

Voice of Freedom
66" x 65", Barbara Temple, Mesa, AZ, 1987. Cottons; hand appliquéd and hand quilted.
1997.06.90

Joyce Ann Tennery

Exploring design and color anew with each quilt she made was the heart of Joyce's artistry. In her lifetime, achievement came about by carrying on the tradition through teaching others and judging.

Night and Noon Variation
72" x 92", Joyce Ann Tennery, Oak Ridge, TN, 1987. Cottons; hand pieced and hand quilted.
1997.06.45

Leureta Beam Thieme

Leureta found self-expression through sewing clothes and creating original clothing designs, and quiltmaking has served as another artistic outlet.

Oriental Poppy
90" x 95", Leureta Beam Thieme, Pasadena, MD, 1987. Polished cottons; machine pieced, hand appliquéd, and hand quilted.
1997.06.51

JUDITH THOMPSON

For more than thirty years I have been interested in textile art. Along with a lifelong interest in history, I developed a special interest in quilts.

By combining piecing, applique, and quilting by hand, I take inspiration from earlier works to evolve my own designs, using traditional techniques I continue to refine. I am especially interested in appliqué because it allows me to freely create and express my ideas in new designs. I prefer hand quilting because it allows fine control of my work.

I enjoy teaching and take great satisfaction as many of my students progress to become accomplished quilters.

My vision is to create new and unique quilts by interpreting vintage works and incorporating combinations of design elements and color layering.

AWARDS:
AQS
Best of Show
1997

VINTAGE ROSE GARDEN
94" x 94½", Judith Thompson, Wenonah, NJ, 1996. Cottons, new and vintage; hand appliquéd, hand pieced, and hand quilted.
1997.04.01

ZENA THORPE

ALABASTER RELIEF
74" x 86", Zena Thorpe, Chatsworth, CA, 2003. Cotton sateen, rayon thread, wool batting; hand appliquéd, embroidered, and quilted.
2005.01.01

William Morris, founder of The Arts and Crafts Movement, believed in integrated creativity and labor.

He said, "That thing which I understand by real art is the expression by man of his pleasure in labor." He argued ceaselessly that there must be satisfaction of creation in the labor that produces goods.

This is a philosophy to which I subscribe and which expresses my hope for achievement in my quiltmaking: the personal satisfaction and pleasure that come from creating something with my heart and hands.

If that something is a piece of art which gives pleasure to others, then that satisfaction is multiplied tenfold.

AWARDS:
AQS
Hand Workmanship
2005

Ricky Tims

I constantly strive to create work that is aesthetically pleasing and that exemplifies the traditions that are historically present in quiltmaking, holding myself to a high standard of workmanship to achieve this.

In pursuit of my quilting craft, I have attempted to create designs that are appealing to the traditional side of quilting but still have characteristics that are reflective of contemporary quilts. When I'm designing things that are traditional, I want them to have a contemporary flair and often use color to accomplish this. I hope that my work honors quilters from centuries past and provides a bridge between the two.

AWARDS:
Bernina
Machine Workmanship
2006

Fire Dragon Rhapsody
60" x 60", Ricky Tims, LaVeta, CO, 2004. Hand-dyed cottons, metallic threads; raw-edge and fusible machine appliqué, trapunto, machine quilted.
2006.05.01

Ricky Tims

Passage

39½" x 49", Ricky Tims, La Veta, CO, 1998. Ricky's own hand dyed 100% cotton fabrics and commercial batiks; machine pieced, machine appliquéd and machine quilted. 2009.03.01

Passage was created for the front cover of a CD. The music was produced and conducted by Ricky and featured a St. Louis community chorus and members of the St. Louis Symphony Orchestra. The album, featuring a requiem, included songs of hope and healing. This quilt expresses the gentleness of passing from this life to another.

He has not left us our dearest love, nor has he traveled far,
Just stepped inside home's loveliest room and left the door ajar.

This quilt was juried into the 1999 AQS Quilt Show and Contest.

MARJORIE D. TOWNSEND

Marjorie's use of quilt-making as an art form was based on years of quilting as a fundamental necessity.

TULIPS IN A BASKET
87" x 108", Marjorie D. Townsend, Parsons, TN, 1984. Cottons; hand appliquéd and hand quilted.
1997.06.87

TRIGG COUNTY QUILTERS

The members of this Cadiz, Kentucky, area quilt guild meet regularly, take trips together, conduct community service projects, and volunteer at The National Quilting Museum.

TRADITION IN THE ATTIC
86½" x 94½", Trigg Co. Quilters, Cadiz, KY, 1988. Cottons; hand pieced and hand quilted.
2000.05.01

LUDMILA USPENSKAYA

As an academically trained artist and designer, I have always created artworks based on my own experiences, surroundings, and ideas.

The artistry of my quilt-making explores the capacity of my creativity and brings quilt-making to the level of high art.

TRADITIONAL BOUQUET
52" x 66", Ludmila Uspenskaya, Brooklyn, NY, 1995. Cottons; machine appliquéd and machine quilted.
1995.01.01

Elsie Vredenburg

I quilt because I love fabric in its many colors and patterns, and I love cutting it up and sewing it back together to make new designs.

Even though I always said I had no artistic talent (translation: ability to draw) and avoided art classes every time I could, I think, deep in my heart, this is what I always longed to be able to do.

I make quilts for enjoyment, both mine and others'. If I like a quilt when it is finished, I am happy. If others like it, too, I am happier.

Amish Easter Baskets
84" x 110", Elsie Vredenburg, Tustin, MI, 1987. Cottons; machine pieced and hand quilted.
1992.14.01

Awards:
Third Place
Theme: Baskets
1988

ELSIE VREDENBURG

ICE FANTASIA
74" x 87", Elsie Vredenburg, Tustin, MI, 1989. Cottons; machine pieced and hand quilted.
1992.10.01

AWARDS:
Second Place
Theme: Fans
1990

Carol Wadley

Sunset Kites
63" x 63", Carol Wadley, Hillsboro, OR, 1985. Cottons; machine pieced and hand quilted.
1997.06.80

I made my first quilt from maternity blouse scraps and children's play clothes, which filled three large grocery bags.

Then I made a quilt for each of our four beds, my brother, sister, and parents.

Next I made two quilts to keep myself busy while my husband was in Vietnam for a year.

After that I discovered quilt shops and all manner of wonderful things just for quilters like classes from all the great quilting teachers, non-juried and juried quilt shows, and publications.

Now, I want to use up my fabric and make all my design sketches and finish up my latest quilt (with my 95-year-old mother) and have the good grace to give some of these quilts away. They're taking up every closet!

DEBRA WAGNER

One of the early proponents of machine quilting, Debra's trademark achievement in the quilting world has been precision machine work.

FLORAL URNS
90" x 90", Debra Wagner, Cosmos, MN, 1992. Cottons; machine pieced, machine appliquéd, machine embroidered, and machine quilted with trapunto.
1996.01.11

AWARDS:
Bernina
Machine Workmanship
1993

DEBRA WAGNER

OHIO BRIDE'S QUILT
81" x 81", Debra Wagner, Cosmos, MN, 1989. Cottons; machine pieced and machine quilted with trapunto.
1997.06.49

AWARDS:
First Place Other Techniques
Viewers' Choice
1990

DEBRA WAGNER

SUNBURST QUILT
90" x 89", Debra Wagner, Cosmos, MN, 1994. Cottons; machine pieced and machine quilted with trapunto.
1996.01.25

AWARDS:
Bernina
Machine Workmanship
1995

DAVID WALKER

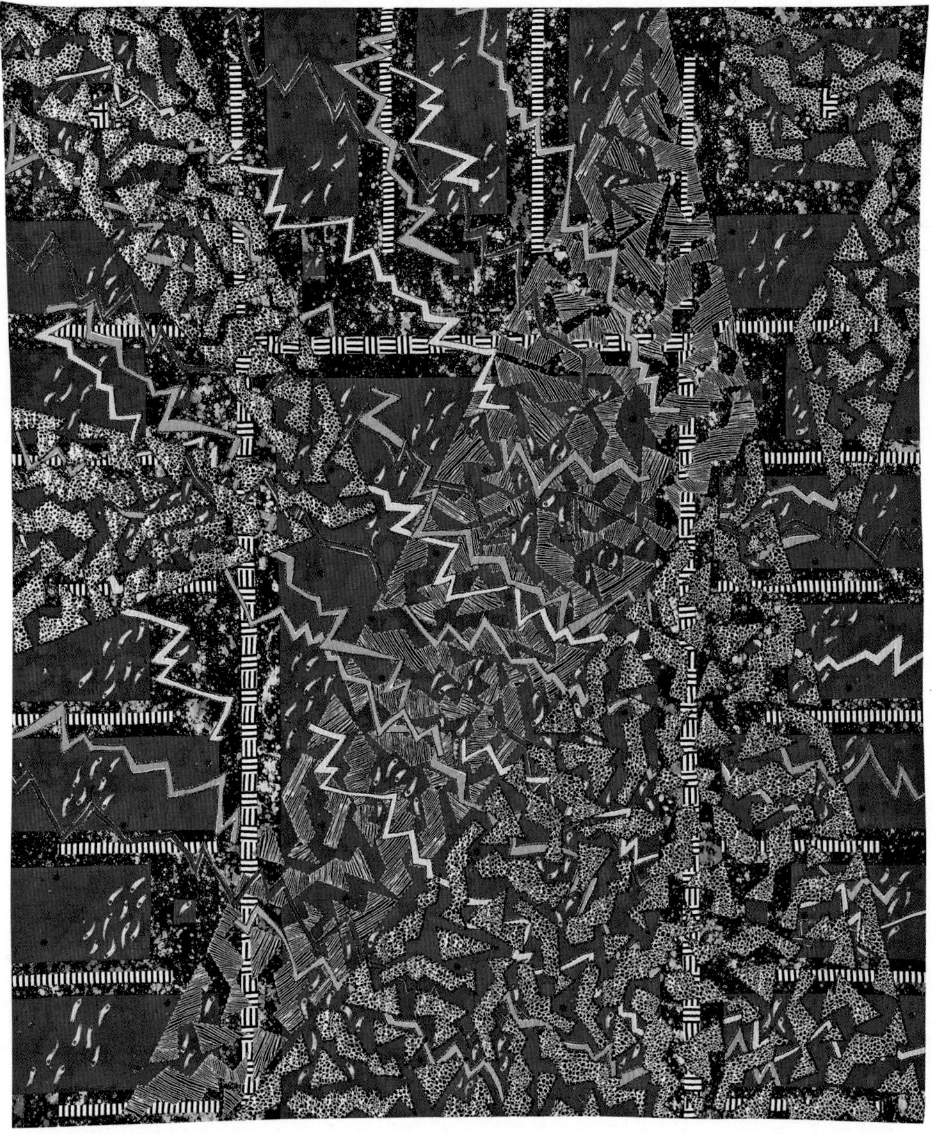

THE OTHER SIDE OF SILENCE
78" x 91", David Walker, Cincinnati, OH, 1989. Cottons, blends, and metallic fabrics; control-bleached and hand-dyed fabrics; cotton and acrylic yarn; beads; sequins, fabric paint; machine pieced and machine appliquéd.
2010.01.01

There is a silence that is so peaceful that it fools us into believing that it defines the quiet place where one meets the Divine. In reality, entering into this silence is only half of the journey because it is beyond this quiet place that we must travel, beyond this place which has lulled us into such a false sense of peace---there we will find journey's true end. We must travel further than the silence to find our way home to universal peace and love. Beyond the silence and prepared by the Ultimate Host, there is a celebration awaiting us---a loud, raucous, energy-packed experience of endless creativity and perfect merriment. If anyone should know how to throw a party, it surely must be the Source of creation itself.

DEBORAH LYNN WARD

In the short period of time Deborah was a quilter before her death, she embraced machine appliqué and quilting techniques and developed a signature style in an impressive body of work for one so young.

NIGHT FLOWERS
60" x 60", Deborah Lynn Ward, Arroyo Grande, CA, 1990. Cottons; machine pieced, machine appliquéd, hand beaded, and machine quilted.
1992.19.01

MARIYA WATERS

RENAISSANCE REVIVAL
86½" x 86½", Mariya Waters, Melbourne, Victoria, Australia, 2008. Cottons, Matilda's Own Cotton/wool blend batting, metallic thread; machine pieced, hand appliquéd, hand couched, machine quilted.
2009.01.01

"This quilt has been a labour of love, a test of skill and patience," writes Mariya Waters. "I did have difficult days and in the latter part of the work it was hard to stay focused, as, like all my bigger quilts, I was seriously 'over it'. Some days I despaired that I would never ever finish the project. My husband, Gavin, even made the comment one day that 'this quilt would get finished even if he had to complete it!' We decided that was not an option because it would then become a group quilt. Gavin then would become my quilt angel and on some days he would do the washing and was often seen doing the ironing. My time each day stretched longer I was often working in excess of 15 hours a day."

AWARDS:
AQS
Best of Show
2009

Collection of The National Quilt Museum

Rachel Wetzler

Breeze
55" x 43½", Rachel Wetzler, St. Charles, IL, 2006. Cottons, polyester sheer, Prismacolor art pencils, Setacdor paints, paint markers, beads, fusible web and interfacing; machine pieced, appliquéd, and quilted; hand embroidered and beaded.
2007.09.01

AWARDS:
Moda
Best Wall Quilt
2007

To safely cross the street, children are taught three words: stop, look, and listen. An exceptional quilt achieves the same three things.

A quilt with strong visual impact stops people in their tracks.

As the viewer looks closely at the quilt, the complexity of design and attention to detail becomes apparent.

If a person takes the time to listen, the quilt will speak to them—sometimes with enough impact to alter their life in some way.

My goal is to honor God by creating quilts that help the viewer stop, look, and listen.

My hope is that they will see and hear beauty and truth.

Anna Williams

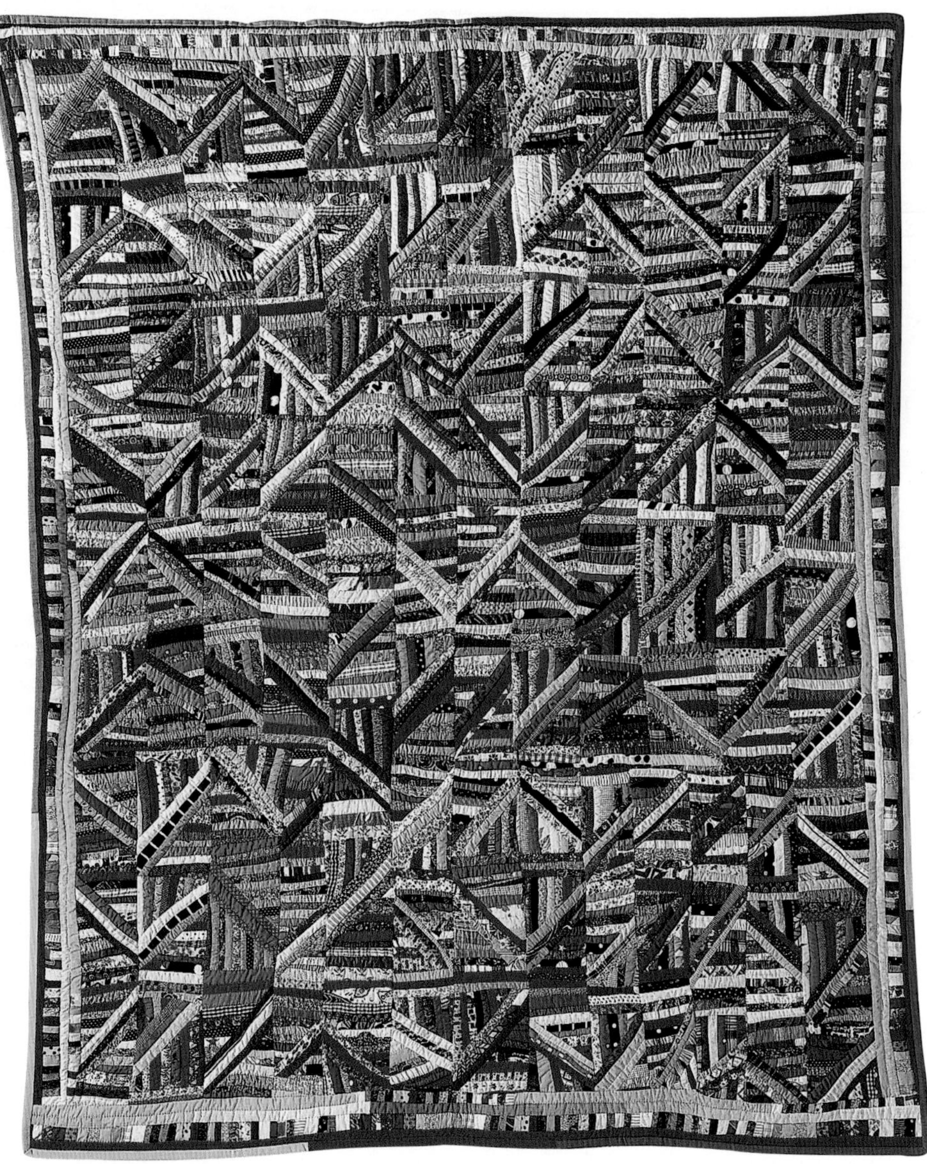

That Anna's improvisational approach to making quilts has unintentionally influenced other quiltmakers surprises her, and what pleases her is that her art is something others enjoy.

A Li'l Bit Crazy Two
63" x 78", Anna Williams, Baton Rouge, LA, 1994; quilted by Mary Walker. Cottons; hand and machine pieced and hand quilted.
2001.09.01

Beverly Mannisto WILLIAMS

Hand quilting gave Beverly a way to express her desire to create lasting works of creativity and artistry.

Though this is an award-winning quilt, Beverly reveals that it includes one flaw. She missed quilting one flower in the center design as she quilted on that January 1986 day the NASA shuttle Challenger exploded. The error was left as a remembrance.

VICTORIAN FANTASY OF FEATHERS AND LACE
89" x 104", Beverly Mannisto Williams, Cadillac, MI, 1986. Cotton, handmade bobbin lace edge; hand quilted with trapunto. National Quilting Association Masterpiece Quilt. 1996.01.29

AWARDS:
Gingher Hand Workmanship
1987

CASSANDRA WILLIAMS

THE MAP MAKERS
56½" x 65", Cassandra Williams, Grants Pass, OR, 2003. Cottons; raw-edge machine appliqué; machine quilted, hand painted and beaded.
2004.03.01

The majority of my quilts depict realistic wildlife and include some traditional piecing.

Having a deep appreciation of traditional quilting, I try to display an area of piecing within my design. However, I'm first and last an artist who needs to create an original work of art.

Working with today's tremendous selection of fabrics stimulates the imagination and makes the creative juices flow.

I hope to pass along my love of animals and inspire others to appreciate their beauty through my work.

By the end of my quilting days, I hope to have inspired a number of quilters to expand their talents to include not only traditional quilts, but other forms of the art.

AWARDS:

Best Quilt Lewis and Clark Expedition Quilts
Nashville, Tennessee
2003

JUDY WOODWORTH

AVATAR REVISITED is a whole cloth black cotton sateen quilt. It took me approximately four months to work on the design, a week or two to transfer it to the black sateen, four to five weeks to quilt, and a week to do the binding using the ladder stitch.

The original pattern was designed in ⅛ miniature and drawn with a mechanical pencil. After it was perfected over the months, I copied this drawing, and saved a second copy so that it could be mirror imaged to become a ¼ of the design. I transferred an enlarged copy to black cotton sateen fabric, using a light box, and marking with Fons and Porter mechanical pencils.

AWARDS:
APQS Longarm Machine Quilting
2012

AVATAR REVISITED
67" x 67", Judy Woodworth, Gering, NE, 2010. Cotton, Fil-tec Glide thread, Legacy 80/20 and Legacy Wool batting; longarm machine quilted.
2012.02.04

KATHY WYLIE

INSTRUMENTS OF PRAISE

69" x 69", Kathy Wylie, Whitby, Ontario, Canada, 2009. Commercial cotton fabric, silk, 60-weight cotton thread, cotton and monofilament threads, embroidery floss, beads, buttons, Sulky Sliver thread, double-strand twisted cord, wool batting, 80/20 cotton/polyester blend batting; machine pieced, hand appliquéd, hand embroidered, hand embellished, machine quilted. Block designs were adapted from a CorelDraw Medieval clipart collection; corner motifs adapted from the Dover book "Victorian Stencils" by Edmund V. Gillon Jr.
2011.03.02

Instruments of Praise was inspired by the words of Psalm 150.

Praise Him with the sounding of the trumpet,
praise Him with the harp and lyre,
praise Him with tambourine and dancing,
praise Him with the strings and flute,
praise Him with the clash of cymbals,
praise Him with resounding cymbals.
Let everything that has breath, praise the Lord.
Praise the Lord.

AWARDS:
Bernina
Machine Workmanship
2011

JUANITA GIBSON YEAGER

What I hope to achieve with the artistry of my quiltmaking is to convey successfully, through the use of shapes abstracted from nature, my love and fascination with color and cloth.

Underlying the bold, large-scale graphic nature of my work is my use of colors that have both seasonal connotations and cultural undertones. I hope I have mastered this aspect of my art well enough that it shows in my work.

Because I consider myself an artist, I want those who see my work to feel my joy and sense my happiness.

To a lesser degree, I want people to see my love of cloth and my respect for the traditional quilts that covered our beds long before they graced our walls.

LILIES OF AUTUMN
70" x 74", Juanita Gibson Yeager, Louisville, KY, 1991. Cottons; hand pieced and hand quilted.
1997.06.32

MARLA YEAGER

BUCKSKIN
78" x 79", Marla Yeager, Ava, MO, 2006. Cottons, hand-dyed cottons, silk thread, nylon monofilament thread; machine pieced, machine quilted.
2007.07.01

Quilts are items of intense passion in our lives and tug at our heartstrings like few other things.

At birth, we are swaddled in a quilt. As a child, we have a "security" quilt. When we get married, we are given a wedding quilt. When we are sick and dying, we are comforted by a quilt.

We can take a trip down memory lane by standing in front of a quilt that carries us back to days of our childhood.

Quilts provide a vehicle for me to inspire our generation to achieve all they can, and to leave a part of myself behind as a visual reminder for future generations of a passion that runs deep in my life and defines who I am.

AWARDS:

Bernina
Machine Workmanship
2007

LOUISE YOUNG

My work has been influenced by indigenous cultures which produce textiles that are not only beautiful, but utilitarian, designed to incorporate art in everyday life.

My goal is to create something decorative and functional. All of my quilts are designed to be used on a bed to provide warmth.

In addition, I emphasize natural products in both the raw materials (batting, fabric, thread) and the tools that I use. Since cotton is one of the most chemically intensive agricultural products in the world, whenever possible, I use organically grown cotton that has been dyed with natural or low-impact dyes.

In this way, I hope that my quilts will not only provide warmth for this generation but for healthy generations in the future.

AWARDS:

First Place

Appliqué, Amateur

1989

SILVERSWORD – DEGENER'S DREAM
92½" x 94", Louise Young, Tioga, PA, 1988. Cottons; hand appliquéd and hand quilted.
1992.06.01

NADENE ZOWADA

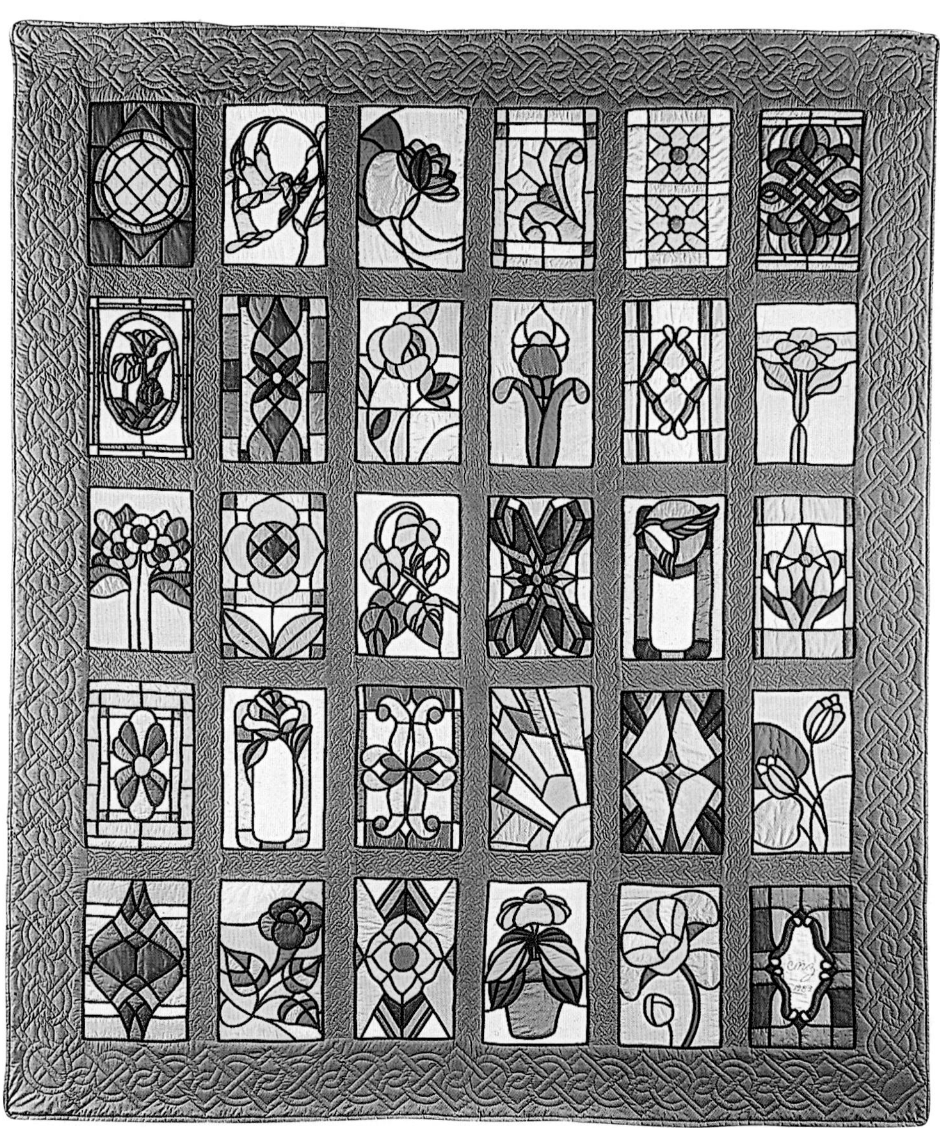

An inherited love of quilting from her mother and grandmother and the opportunity to devote a lot of time to quilting afforded through long winters in the Big Horn Mountains fueled the late Nadene's artistry and achievements.

STAINED GLASS WINDOWS
98" x 112", Nadene Zowada, Buffalo, WY, 1983. Cotton/polyester; hand appliquéd and quilted.
1997.06.73

INDEX

MUSEUM ACTIVITIES